"I love this book! From long-time artist, teacher, and seeker, Janice Mason Steeves, *Bloom, On Becoming an Artist Later in Life* is an encyclopedia of the soul's journey into creativity, authenticity, healing and wholeness. Every chapter is a consciousness-transforming meditation and inspirational guide welcoming the unfinished self into its hidden potential and ultimate blossoming. I believe this book is destined to become a bestseller in the tradition of Julia Cameron's classic, *The Artist's Way*. If you are an artist, aspiring artist, or art lover, may I introduce your personal mentor."

—John C. Robinson, Ph.D., D.Min.
Aging with Vision, Hope and Courage in a Time of Crisis

Bloom

On
Becoming
An Artist
Later in Life

Janice Mason Steeves

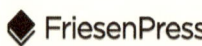 FriesenPress

One Printers Way
Altona, MB R0G 0B0
Canada

www.friesenpress.com

Edited by Jen Mason and Marjorie Anderson

Cover design by Andrew Mason

ISBN
978-1-03-918236-3 (Hardcover)
978-1-03-918235-6 (Paperback)
978-1-03-918237-0 (eBook)

1. ART, INDIVIDUAL ARTISTS, ESSAYS

Distributed to the trade by The Ingram Book Company

To those who respond to the calling of their creative souls.
May you bloom.

Table of Contents

Part I
Coming to Art
Later in Life

Introduction

It's never too late to be what you might have been.
—George Eliot

There is a timing for things. It isn't a mistake or a sign of weakness when a person waits until later in life to become an artist. It's just that the time hasn't been right for them to do so any earlier. Like late-blooming plants.

In nature, most plants and trees bloom in the spring and summer, but certain ones are ready to flower only in the late fall or winter. In Southern Ontario, where I live, some fall and winter-blooming plants are goldenrod, oxeye daisy, snow drops, witch hazel and sedum. The magnificent saguaro cactus, which grows in the Sonoran Desert between Arizona and Mexico, can live for 150-200 years, but only blooms after thirty-five years. The Madagascar palm tree blooms with hundreds of tiny flowers only once in one hundred years. Likewise, the enormous and stunning corpse flower, native to the island of Sumatra in Indonesia, blooms only once in one hundred years.

I bloomed late too. I came to art as a total beginner after working for years in educational psychology. I had to overcome many personal barriers and limitations. I had to learn to take myself seriously as an artist, to establish personal boundaries, to have the courage to continue in the face of objections, and to trust that I was on the right path. I had to gain the confidence to call myself an artist.

3

Along the way, I often wondered, 'how is it that people, predominantly women, come to art later in life?' and, in 2015, that wonder turned into the seed of this book. One morning, in an artist residency in Sweden, I awoke with the clear memory of a dream. I'm someone who rarely remembers her dreams, and while this was only a fragment, a flash of an image, it stayed with me. I knew what it meant. In the dream, I saw myself standing in front of a group of older people, talking to them about a book I had just written on coming to art later in life. That was, I know now, this book.

It's been a long, complicated path to follow the direction of that dream and write this book. In the early stages, I wrote to artists I knew to ask for their stories. A few years later, in 2019, I wrote a post for my Facebook timeline inviting artists over age sixty to share the stories of their artistic journeys. I indicated that I was writing a book and thought it would be encouraging and inspiring to read about the journeys to art others have taken. I sent a questionnaire to all 168 artists who responded to this social media post. Besides asking for general information like age, location, what work they did before they retired, and how old they were when they came to art, I included a few open-ended questions:

- What were the challenges they faced?

- Were there any regrets about not starting art earlier in life?

- What benefits have there been in coming to art later in life?

- What life lessons has art taught them.

I received 138 responses. Of these, 122 were women, sixteen were men, and all were between the ages of fifty-six and seventy-nine, most between sixty-three and sixty-nine. The majority of those who responded were from Canada and the United States, but there were also responses from Switzerland, Australia, Ireland, England, France, Belgium, Mexico, Germany, and Northern Cyprus. All respondents had previously been employed or still worked, and their type of employment covered a wide variety of jobs: urban planner, medical researcher, cable installer, social worker, bank personnel manager, teacher, nurse, mining camp cook, and flower farmer. One woman had been a gill-net salmon fisher who owned her own boat. Another is a Christmas tree farmer and this seasonal business provides extra income for her art practice. Some have had multiple careers. Magdalena Groszek, for example, an artist living part time in both Spain and France, studied medicine, worked in the financial markets, qualified and worked as a psychotherapist, and obtained degrees in both psychology and yoga therapy.

Reading through the artists' responses, I found answers to my question about why people come to art later in life. Some respondents come to art searching for deeper meaning in their lives, searching for the sunlight to bring alive the seeds of self-expression that grow in their souls. Some come to fill their time in retirement, then, a door opens. That door opened for me when I took my first art class and the ground beneath my feet moved. I couldn't sleep because of the excitement I felt. For some respondents, the desire to create was there earlier in their lives, but it was not supported by a teacher who made discouraging comments, or it was disallowed by parents who directed them to focus on what could earn them a living.

There is a growing body of knowledge and research related to the phenomenon of creativity surging in the latter part of our lives. We're at a key moment in history, Sara Lawrence-Lightfoot points out in her book, *The Third Chapter: Passion, Risk, and Adventure in the 25 years after 50*. Demographers are recognizing the significance of a distinct developmental phase—those years following early adulthood and middle age when we're neither young nor old. This "third chapter," the author goes on to say "is a stage in life when many women and men are embracing new challenges and searching for greater meaning in life."[1]

This book is about spending our time in the 'third chapter' to become an artist—to find, hone, and share one's creative voice. It's about the benefits, challenges, and lessons of blooming—like the

Madagascar palm—with the maturity and beauty of a life largely lived. This book is divided into parts according to the questions I asked the respondents and then into chapters based on the answers they gave to these questions. I included quotations from the artists as well as some inspiring and deeply personal stories some have shared with me with their permission. Along with these stories, I included some of my own, as well as inspirational stories of other older women I know or have read about. While I focus on the artistic discipline of painting, which is my area and that of many of the artists who responded to my questionnaire, the words and thoughts apply to any artistic focus.

In Part I, I discuss my own journey to art; how the desire for self-expression guided English artist, Diana Kerswell's life; and the stories of two older artists, Doris McCarthy and a woman I'll call Mary, who have inspired me.

In Part II, I present the benefits of coming to art later in life. Joy was often mentioned as an advantage according to the respondents, as was the gift of finding community with others through the shared interest of art, and the opportunity to travel with other like-minded souls. While art has long been known as a form of healing, it came as another unexpected benefit to some of the artists. But the most important benefit by far, was the opportunity to continue to learn and grow and through that, to know themselves better.

Part III describes some of the challenges respondents have faced. While late-in-life artists have developed a great deal of confidence simply by having lived and overcome endless difficulties and experiences, the first challenge that they reported was self-doubt. Other challenges involved taking themselves seriously and allowing themselves the space and time to practise their art; the difficult issue of changing their identity—moving from the role that family and friends have come to know—to someone else: artist. Respondents reflected on the challenge of learning to finding their own artistic voices and about the issue of time and how much time is left in our lives to learn and explore. They discussed fear and the courage that is necessary to become an artist, especially later in life. Finally, the section concludes with respondents musing on the topic of regret.

In Part IV, I share a number of ways to support the practice of art. As an artist with forty years of experience and as someone who has taught and mentored artists from Canada, the USA, Australia, England, Scotland, Sweden, Iceland and Norway for fifteen years, I have found that there are some key practices that support artists on their journey. Unlike many painting teachers, my focus is less about imparting how-to knowledge regarding specific techniques (although technique is important) and more about mindset, orientation, and the inner work of art. The first most important of these is to learn the craft, do the work, put in the time—assisted by focusing on creating a series (creating several paintings with a similar theme or way of painting) using the power of limits to help us make choices and developing our work and ourselves in a deeper way, instead of exploring all possibilities available to us. Some artists and musicians speak of getting into the space or the flow, a place we all wish to inhabit while we create. While meditation and mindfulness can help somewhat with that process, others have rituals they use to begin work that help them get in the flow. Other supporting practices include enabling trust in ourselves and in our work; committing to our practice; learning about the often ignored power of silence as a tool in composition; recognizing the importance of play to generate ideas and not take ourselves too seriously; giving ourselves permission to be imperfect; and empowering ourselves with the discipline to show up consistently in our studios.

Part V is the powerful surprise conclusion, at least it was for me. According to the majority of respondents, the most important benefit of art was not to learn to paint or express themselves or to have a community with whom to show their work, but *to know themselves better*. This was echoed in their responses about the lessons of coming to art: including insights about surrender, patience, authenticity and learning to live with paradox which also led to self-knowledge. These unexpected responses led me to consider the possibility that art is, or can be, a training ground for becoming elders in our society. Elders are not simply those who live to an old age, but rather, are those who have maturity and wisdom, who know themselves, who love and appreciate the planet and whose orientation includes an emphasis on service and care-taking the world, or at least an aspect of it.

In the final chapter, I reflect further on the notion of eldering and shifting current ideas about what it means to be old. I hope that this book plays a role in acknowledging the power of older people, that it demonstrates how older people can move with confidence and passion into a creative stage of life, where they can continue to learn and grow and contribute in an important way in this world, unconcerned with what others think of them. I want to acknowledge how older artists are opening up to a new stage of life, turning inward and outward at the same time, and getting to know ourselves on a much deeper level. Through art, we may grow into the role of elder. This role is essential in our society, providing stability and depth, wisdom-keeping, space-holding, and care-taking.

If there is a creative call inside of you, at any level of volume, it is my hope that this book will inspire you to heed it, regardless of your age. When we wholeheartedly follow the yearning to create, a door opens into an unknown place. We uncover parts of ourselves we have never known; we allow our souls to have expression. Art becomes our teacher, our friend, our joy. It can also be our frustration and maybe, occasionally, our enemy. But most of all, it becomes our mentor. Once we say 'yes' to it, we are on the journey. There is no turning back. If we give our hearts to it, it will give us back a deeper version of ourselves. We meet ourselves anew. We bloom.

Chapter 1:
Finding the Muse

If you want to be an artist, you just need yourself and the nerve to stand up there. For God's sake, if you want to do a thing, just go do it.
—Ray Bradbury

Old age is like climbing a mountain. You climb from ledge to ledge. The higher you get, the more tired and breathless you become, but your views become more extensive.
—Ingmar Bergman

I remember it clearly. It was a September evening in London, Ontario. My friend had talked me into taking a weekly pottery class with her at a local high school. Neither of us had taken a pottery class before. My goal was to learn to make a mug. Our enthusiastic instructor was a well-known local potter. I don't recall that he taught us any specific skills; instead, the gift he gave us was appreciating everything we did. We were allowed to use the four pottery wheels that were in the corner of the classroom, but we had only observed the instructor using a wheel and had no idea how to work it. We just began. I threw the ball of clay into the centre of the wheel and then stepped on the electric pedal just as I had seen the instructor do. I lost control of the ball of clay and it flew onto the floor. I tried again, getting frustrated but starting over again, losing track of time until someone would tap on my shoulder to have his or her turn at the wheel.

The instructor would run over and literally squeal with delight at our most basic efforts. His enthusiasm was infectious. I was so energized after each pottery class that I could barely sleep at night. My friend had the opposite reaction. She lost interest in the class and didn't finish out the term. She had studied interior design in university, so perhaps her creativity had already been unleashed and this was old hat for her. I ended up going by myself to the rest of the classes and then signed up for a second term. I was hooked.

Years went by. I became a potter of sorts, purchasing a wheel and kiln, entering my work in art sales and shows. I had no ability, though, to produce functional pottery, like the mugs I had originally intended to create. I seemed unable to make two mugs or casserole dishes that matched. After fifteen years of trying to make functional pottery, and becoming discouraged with the technical requirements of making glazes, I welcomed the suggestion of another friend to take a watercolour painting class at our local art college. I experienced a reaction similar to the one I had when taking my first pottery class: sleepless nights. I was once again exhilarated to discover another form of creativity, one that felt even closer to my heart. I didn't plan to, but I stopped making pottery almost instantly and never went back to it.

As excited and enthusiastic as I was, I simply never believed that I could become an artist. There was a distant Scottish aunt in my family who was a painter, but none of us knew a thing about her. We didn't know any artists and never once visited an art gallery. Art as I knew it then was either paint-by-numbers (which I loved to do), or pictures of paintings in textbooks, done by European men. It wasn't that I was discouraged from becoming an artist, or that I suppressed my own inclination, it just wasn't an option to be considered.

In my night school watercolour class, I discovered my joy in creativity. And beyond that, it was as though I had come home. In the book, *Spiritual Ecology: The Cry of the Earth*, depth psychologist Bill Plotkin writes, "the first time you consciously inhabit your ultimate place and act from your soul is the first time you can say 'Here' and really know what it means. You've arrived at last, at your own center."[2] I was ecstatic just to watch the magic of colours blending together on the paper. I came home from each class feeling full of creativity, full of delight that something inside me had opened into a world of imagination at a level I hadn't encountered before. It was as though I had stepped through the closet in *The Lion, the Witch and the Wardrobe*, into a kingdom of magic.

This experience bordered on the mystical for me. In all the time I was in university (I spent five years there, earning an M.A. in Clinical Psychology), I never once lost track of time in my studies or felt that I was moving in the realm of something greater than myself. I did feel that in painting, though, and wanted to continue to experience that magic.

I began painting every day, using the kitchen table as my temporary studio workspace, clearing it off at mealtimes. A couple of years after my first painting class, I applied to study art therapy and, at the same time, applied for a leave of absence from my job in school psychology. I wasn't doing this for the money. I was clearly told that I wouldn't receive a higher salary as an art therapist if I was to stay working for the school board. Rather, I was aiming to make my job more interesting. I was accepted into an Art Therapy program, but just a few months before I was to begin, I received a phone call from the Executive Director of the program, telling me that the course had changed entirely in order to be accredited by the American Art Therapy Association. The fees had increased by several thousand dollars, I'd have to go for two years instead of one as had been agreed upon since I already had an M.A., and I'd have to write and defend a thesis. I felt like I'd been kicked in the stomach. I withdrew my application. When I finally recovered from the shock, I decided to take the leave of absence from my job in psychology anyway and see if I had the discipline required to be a full-time artist. Knowing that I had a year to figure out a plan, I worked diligently. At the end of that year, I had my plan. I decided to leave my job for a while at least, and see if I could become an artist. I had to convince myself that I could do it while trying to handle the inner critical voice saying that I couldn't possibly be an artist, I wasn't talented, and didn't start out early enough in life. I felt very much alone at that stage, because it seemed that no one believed in me or understood that I was serious about my art. Eventually, my children grew up to become my biggest supporters but back then, they were young and interested in their own worlds. What sustained me was art itself, the act of creation.

One lesson I've learned through my journey in art and in life, is to say yes.

I don't seem to receive guidance in the form of a small quiet voice in my head. One way it comes instead is through the voices of friends. It seems like my job then, is to hear that guidance, check in with myself and if it feels right, to say yes, as scary as that might be. Such was the case when my friend suggested we take a pottery class together and, years later, when my other friend suggested we take the watercolour class.

The messenger isn't always a friend. After I'd been painting for a few years and was feeling shy about showing my paintings to anyone other than family, one of the mothers at my daughter's school invited parents to have a sale of their arts and crafts to raise money for the school. I worked diligently that winter getting my paintings ready for the sale. When I called the woman in the spring to find out the date of the sale, she was abrupt and dismissive, saying that she'd decided not to go ahead with the event. I told her how disappointed I was and that I'd worked all winter on the project. "What sort of painting do you do?" she asked. I told her I worked in watercolour. "Oh I hate watercolour," she replied. I was shocked, speechless, and angry. I told a friend, who encouraged me to show the work in my home. Spurred on by my anger, I agreed. My friend created beautiful invitations in calligraphy (there were no personal computers then) and I invited fifty friends.

On the day of my home show, I was so nervous that I had a debilitating migraine, something I had never had before. But, the show went on and was a success. It sold out! I learned a valuable lesson which was to turn disappointment or rejection into an opportunity. The woman's dismissive behaviour was a huge catalyst in helping me turn my anger into something positive.

The next really big push came from Elizabeth Bard, whom I had hired to help me in my garden. She was helping me take out some dead juniper bushes next to my studio window. An accomplished artist who painted still life and birds, Elizabeth wanted to try abstraction. I'd been painting and showing my work in galleries for twenty-five years by that time. She looked in the window of my studio and must have been inspired because she asked me if I taught painting classes. I told her that I didn't and in fact had no intention of teaching. Each time I ran into her, she would ask me when I was going to start teaching. Eventually, I reluctantly agreed. I figured if I was going to teach her, I'd see if I could get a few more participants so I sent out emails to some of my artist friends and the class filled in a couple of days. That led slowly… slowly, to my teaching art classes in local art centres, then in art schools across Canada and the US, to teaching painting work-shops internationally and on Zoom, and, most recently, to creating my international workshop project: Workshops in Wild Places. This project of leading small groups of artists to remote and wild places both internationally and in Canada has become a huge delight for me. My intention is to facilitate these artists in making a deeper connec-tion with the land, to fall back in love with the Earth, and to use this as inspiration for their work.

While my teaching focus has evolved considerably over the years into a much larger vision, so has my style of painting. I painted in a representational way for twenty-five years, trying various mediums like encaustic and acrylics before settling on working in oil paint. I exhibited my work in juried shows, winning awards and grants, and eventually found representation in five galleries across Canada. The most challenging step in my art journey, though, was not going to art school or finding gallery representation: it was moving from painting in a representational way to painting abstractly or non-objectively. There were a couple of events that happened to encourage me to make this transition. An artist at one of my art openings commented on one of my vessel paintings in the exhibition. It had a heavily textured fabric-like background. She encouraged me to drop the image and work with just the background. The other change was learning how to use cold wax medium mixed with oil paint. It has a wonderful butter-like consistency that I could layer and cut back into, creating textures. I was ready for a change. I didn't feel as though my representational painting was expressing the depth of what I wanted to say. I wanted to speak about the essence of a thing and not be limited by form.

Little did I know that this decision would plunge me into one of the most difficult, soul-searching times of my life. I decided to leave behind all the well-known touchstones in my work—light, form, beauty—and head off into uncharted territory. To say that it was personally terrifying will sound inane, but it was though I had descended into a dark labyrinth. There, in the darkness, I wrestled with a powerful force that wanted to stay in a comfortable place, that didn't want to move forward. In that darkness were lessons about courage, patience, and determination. I worked seven days a week, fifteen hours a day for many months, trying to find my way into abstraction. I wondered if I ever would, not knowing what I was searching for and afraid that I would not be able to recognize it if I did find it.

Giving up an image sounds easy, but as someone who had painted images for twenty-five years, I felt as if the ground had fallen away from under my feet. The ways I had previously planned my compositions—deciding where to place images in the picture frame, how to paint light moving over the images, choosing what colours to put into the shadows—were gone. I was jumping off a cliff. Blindfolded. I had no images, no light, no form, no shadows. In short, I had no limitations, no known reference point. I had complete freedom. There's a puzzling thing about having complete freedom—where does one begin to paint when there are no limitations, no parameters?

Art is a path. It's a spiritual path if you choose it to be. That summer, I knew I was on a serious creative and spiritual path. It would involve nothing less than everything. And once I had committed to it, I felt as though there was no turning back.

Chapter 2:
Desire for Self-Expression

Life isn't about finding yourself.
Life is about creating yourself.
—George Bernard Shaw

Art calls us with a fierce intensity to develop a relationship with our soul. It's a powerful need that finds satisfaction only in our creative efforts. Our connection to art might have been suppressed early on by parents, by thoughtless words from teachers, or from life taking us in other directions, but the longing for it always remains. In his book, *Stoking the Creative Fires, 9 Ways to Rekindle Passion and Imagination,* Phil Cousineau describes that intense desire for self-expression as a "gold thread [that runs] from your soul to your real work. Hold onto it for dear life."[3] Cousineau goes on to write about the Oregon poet William Stafford who speaks of a mythic thread of destiny woven by the Three Fates: "There's a thread you follow. It goes among things that change. But it doesn't change. You don't ever let go of the thread."[4]

I have heard that desire for artistic expression in the voices of my students and in the words of the artists who responded to my questionnaire. Some of those responses spurred me on to email the artists for more information. One artist I contacted was Diana Kerswell, an artist from England.

Diana is someone who has held steadfastly to her gold thread. Determination and desire drove her from an early age. She had wanted to become an artist from childhood, encouraged by her grandfather and her aunt; however, her father believed that artists didn't earn a good living and, therefore, wouldn't allow her to study art. He told her that if she applied for a secretarial course she could study art on the side. But after she was accepted for the secretarial course, her father went back on his word, refusing to allow her to study art and refusing to pay for her education. He told her she should go out and get a job as he had done at the same age. In frustration, Diana ran away from home at age sixteen. In the following years, she married, worked as a secretary and soon began a family. Thirteen years later, she tried again to go to art school:

> I was accepted to do a Foundation course at an art school, which I did, but I found it hard to adjust to being a student and did not really get as much out of it as I could have. My four children were all under the age of eight years and I had three-year-old twins and a divorce. That's not an excuse but it did make it harder, and impossible to go on to a degree at that time.

She held fast to her gold thread, and the creative drive never subsided in her. She went to art school part-time over many years while she worked in the television industry, finally graduating with a Fine Arts degree in 2001 at age fifty-six. About her life, Diana, now seventy-five, says:

> I had to overcome the prohibitions of my father about being an artist. In fact, I owe him my determination to become an artist, as I always felt that I would show him one day. And I was very angry for a very long time. I just refused to give up until I got to where I felt confident, which is what doing the Fine Arts degree did for me. In spite of doing many different jobs—typing, working in a hat shop, being an artist's model, a legal clerk, a [television]

subtitler, a mother, an art therapist/psychotherapist—I was still determined I would get there one day.

American respondent, Jeanette Cook describes how the desire for artistic self-expression arrived suddenly and unexpectedly in a modern dance class and never left her:

> I grew up in a Catholic, ranching family in New Mexico. I was the only girl out of five children. As it was for all of us at this time, the only expectation was to get married and have kids. I wanted to take art classes but no, I had to take music and dance, to better able my prospects of marriage. Well I couldn't sing (tone deaf) and I had my fingers hit regularly with a stick by the nuns for striking the wrong keys on the piano. That left dance, which I took on with intensity. At 23, I was the first of my family to graduate from college, with a BFA degree in Theatre Arts, with a Dance emphasis. Much to the horror of my parents, I moved to New York City to become a famous dancer. I knew no one in NYC, being a country girl, I soon found the expansive NYC library, dance instructors I loved, and gay boys who dressed me up and took me out. Two years after moving to the Big Apple, I took a modern dance class at the 92nd Street Y. At the end of class the instructor said, 'Let's improv on this final combination.' Fifty students moved across the floor once and half dropped out, once more across even more dropped out. Musicians were coming in for the next rehearsal and setting up. Two bongo players, a sax, a bass player and a couple of horns all started improving with us. At this point there were only three dancers left on the floor, all of us in tune to what was happening with the movement and music. Spontaneously and intuitively, four minutes later, the dance came to a conclusion. We were all amazed at what had just happened

and everyone in the room felt the power of the event. We all shook hands and acknowledged the moment. The musicians continued warming up and I walked out of the 92nd St. Y with the other dancer. She got on the train to go uptown and I got on the train downtown.

Later on, I followed an abusive womanizer to California. I was performing, teaching dance at community colleges, and choreographing for children's theatre. I was in a dangerous terrible relationship and I realized I needed help but by this time I had two children so I moved home to New Mexico and had to find a way to support my kids. I went back to school to become a nurse and then a midwife. By the time I was ready to return to dance my instrument (body) was past its prime for dance. That's when I started to draw and then paint. Figurative drawing and landscape painting for me are like taking ballet, you're learning the technique and discipline, but abstract painting is putting it all together and improvising. I now paint like I danced—in the moment. I find composing an abstract painting to be complex, most of the time it's a struggle, hard work, and can't be forced. Finding the rhythms and patterns out of the chaos of my life is how I strive to paint. No regrets, I was honored and humbled to respectfully care for women and children.

My story, *was* the class in NYC at the 92nd street Y, where in an instant I recognized how to live life in the moment and improvise. It was pivotal to my thinking process, in how I would live the rest of my life. My paintings are complex, often chaotic and I strive for the rhythms and patterns of an improvised choreographed two-dimensional surface. Always searching for that moment at the Y where it all comes together in exquisite beauty and clarity.

David Skillicorn is an American artist whose engagement with painting also began as bolt of lightning. Twenty years ago, the Emmy-award-winning documentary filmmaker, was shooting a film about five visual artists on Cape Cod, Massachusetts. As he looked through his camera lens at one of the artists painting the early morning landscape in delicate, simple brushstrokes, Skillicorn had an epiphany. He said, "I remember thinking as I looked through my lens filming him paint, 'I could do that!' And then, in rapid succession, 'I HAVE to do that!' He says, "I was bitten." Skillicorn has since become a full-time painter who eventually moved into painting non-objectively and now exhibits widely. Fiercely independent, Skillicorn says, "Life is short, and I'm not interested in just rotely producing things. If the challenge and mystery are gone, it isn't worth pursuing."

Coming to art any time in life is a gift. Coming to it later in life is a bonus because we see life through different eyes than when we were young. We're willing to ask anything—no matter if it seems silly—to take risks, to make mistakes. We feel the pressure of time more acutely, which drives our passion and intensifies our focus. "Art did not seem to be a viable path back in the 60s," said American respondent James Edward Scherbarth. "Also as the eldest of seven children" he went on, "finances were always a concern." Needing a job and looking for adventure, James enlisted in the US Army, and ended up serving in Vietnam. He briefly considered pursuing art when he returned, but he was suffering from PTSD (he later realized). He needed to become healthy and find work, so art was put on the back-burner. At age fifty-nine, after twenty-eight years of working in the telecommunications industry, James took an early retirement. One year later, he signed up for a painting class and immediately recommitted himself to his life-long dream. He felt that he was playing catch up which motivated him to be focused, take risks, and just go for it. A few years ago, before he died in 2021, he wrote to say that in committing to painting, he didn't have anything to lose and a great deal to gain. Some, he said, will talk about second chances. He understood that this was not a second chance—that this *was* his chance. Everything that happened in life, he said, was his schooling and that he just spent a bit more time in 'school' than most." James fulfilled his dream. He showed his work in galleries, and was a well-loved art teacher traveling to teach in the US, France and Ireland.

This desire to create sometimes arrives early in life and sometimes is sidetracked for a time, but once touched by it, we never forget it, and it propels us to express ourselves as boldly and honestly as we can, to find our authentic selves. "There is a force within you that breathes divine fire and brings your work to life,[5]" writes Phil Cousineau. I understand exactly what Cousineau means because I can't live without my daily dose of creativity. (When my daughter lived at home, I remember her telling me when I was grumpy that I should just go and paint.) This kind of inner creative fire is shared by others. It's called *duende*. Cousineau explains it in these terms:

> It lifts your spirit, then flings you like a flaming arrow, full of passion and resolve to set the world on fire. This is the blood surge that can be detected in the poems of Federico Lorca, the paintings of Edvard Munch and the dances of Martha Graham. And it's combustible.[6]

Somehow, as I read these words and Lorca's poems aloud in my workshop in Spain, Lorca's birthplace, the words themselves felt like they were burning through me, shooting like arrows straight into everyone's hearts. They made us gasp with their power. Once burned by the fire of expression, it stays in your blood and can never be extinguished.

Chapter 3:
Ageless Creativity

I never feel age...if you have creative work,
you don't have age or time.
—Louise Nevelson

Creativity can flourish no matter our age. Sometimes we hold an ember of creativity from an early age, and it suddenly catches fire as we grow older. In this chapter, I share the stories of two inspiring older women and their creativity. The first was a woman I'll call Mary who was a psychologist in a psychiatric hospital in Ontario where I had just begun to work after university. She was a formidable boss. I'd just finished testing one of the psychiatric patients from the ward I worked on and, with my limited background in assessment but with the confidence of youth, I wrote up a report. Soon after, I received a call in my office from Mary:

"Did you know that you're supposed to speak to me about the test results *before* you write a report?"

"No I didn't," I said. "No one told me that."

"Well, *I'm* telling you that," she replied sternly. "Would you please come down to my office with the test results?"

Mary was like that. Very clear and direct, and she incited fear in the clinicians she mentored. I soon learned, though, that she meant no malice, that she was more bluster than bite. Two years later, when my husband finished graduate school, I left the job and we moved away. For years, Mary and I kept in touch with short messages in our annual Christmas cards. They eventually dropped off. Thirty years later, out of the blue, I heard from her again. By then Mary was in her 90s. She had called one of my galleries to get in touch with me. When I called her, I asked how she'd managed to find me.

"Jan," she said, "I googled you."

I chuckled.

"What are you laughing at?" She still had that direct manner... and was still intimidating.

"Just comparing you to my Mum," I said, "Mum has no idea how to use a computer."

Mary and I resumed our friendship. She remained sharp and quick and still somewhat daunting, though. Once every summer we met for lunch along with another woman, who had worked at the hospital when I did. At the age of ninety-nine, Mary sold her house and moved into a retirement home, having only recently retired from all her volunteer jobs, including teaching an occasional university class on aging. That gave her time to work on a book about her life in the army, where she worked as a psychologist. Her job at the time was to do psychological testing on women recruits to determine their capabilities to work in the war. That first book was published when she was 100. I loved her flamboyant attitude toward life. Always concerned about her appearance, even at 99, she regularly had her nails done, dyed her hair flaming red, and carefully chose her outfits, often wearing leopard print blouses or scarves. At 100, just after she published her book, Mary developed a large tumour in her abdomen. In telling me the story, Mary said that the doctors gave her three choices: Incredibly, the first choice they offered her was euthanasia. The second choice was chemotherapy; the third, surgery. Mary chose surgery. She chose life. She was not ready to give up. It was the correct choice. The tumour, while large, was benign.

Her second book, about her life as a travelling psychologist, was published when she was 102. By then her vision was failing, and she couldn't see the letters on the computer screen. In her ever-resourceful way, Mary hired a secretary to take notes that she dictated for a third book, which, unfortunately, she wasn't able to complete. She died after a brief illness at 103.

Another inspiring creative woman in my life was the famous Canadian landscape painter Doris McCarthy. I met Doris when she was the guest artist at a painting workshop held in Pangnirtung on Baffin Island in Canada's Arctic. A year later, at the exhibition of her paintings from that trip, I lined up to get her autograph on her first autobiography, *A Fool in Paradise*. When she autographed my copy of her book, we talked about Baffin Island, and I told her a story I'd heard from a woman who had spent a winter in Pond Inlet (now called by its Inuit name, Mittimatalik). The woman told me she'd heard that if you see the northern lights and talk to them, they will come down to you. She was determined to try. One night when the northern lights were bright in the sky, she went out into the snowy Arctic night a little way down the road from the house she was staying in. She talked to them as they were slowly swaying and shifting and changing colours in the night sky. I don't know what she said to them but all of a sudden, she had the strange sensation that they were coming down to her. She panicked and ran back to her house. When I told this story to Doris, she looked at me with her pixie smile and said, "Well dear, let's go."

I jumped at the chance to travel with Doris to Baffin Island in the dark January winter. Mittimitalik is on the northern edge of Baffin Island, sitting at the entrance to the Northwest Passage, opposite the famous Bylot Island. It's within the Arctic Circle, which means twenty-four hours of darkness at that time of year. Doris was eighty-two then and while she was still strong and full of energy, I imagined that part of the reason I was there was to help her with her bags and otherwise assist her. Wrong. She threw her bags up onto the pickup truck (aka taxi) before I could get my own up there. She painted for at least five hours or more every day and happily suited up in heavy down pants and coat to go for a walk with me in the -40C temperatures: a dynamo. We had a hilarious and unforgettable time those two weeks in the Arctic, which included a dog sled trip out to an iceberg frozen in the bay. We chipped off a little of the ice to put in our before-dinner drinks: single malt for me, rye for Doris, with ten-thousand-year-old ice cubes.

Because Doris was quite well-known in the village, having visited and painted there for many years, we had permission to stay in the small unused Catholic Church. My bed was in the Narthex under a mural of Jesus in the Arctic, his arms outstretched in welcome. I slept well being blessed each night. Sadly though, we didn't see any northern lights.

While Doris began to paint early in life, she devoted her time to earning a living teaching art to high school students in Toronto, painting as she could in her off hours and weekends. Her art began to really move ahead once she retired at age sixty-five. Although she was then able to focus full time on her art, she decided she wanted to obtain a BA degree (you didn't have to have a BA to teach in those days). She enrolled as a part-time student at the University of Toronto, graduating when she was seventy-nine and later earning five honorary doctorates from five different Canadian Universities as well as inductions into the Order of Ontario (1992) and the Order of Canada (1986). Her place in the canon of great Canadian artists was solidified.

A passionate writer, Doris penned three autobiographies chronicling her life: *A Fool in Paradise, The Good Wine,* and her last book, *Ninety Years Wise,* published when she was ninety-four. Doris died in 2010 at the age of 100.

The lives of these two women, Mary and Doris, are testaments to the fact that creativity doesn't have a timeline associated with it. It can flourish at any age.

Part II
Coming to Art
Later in Life:
Benefits

Chapter 4:
Joy

Grateful people are joyful people;
the more joyful people are, the more
we'll have a joyful world.
—Brother David Steindl-Rast

When asked about one important aspect of coming to art later in life, respondents were clear:

- "Pure unadulterated joy." (Sue Smith, Canada)

- "Total enjoyment. I am happier than I have ever been since I am living my dream. I'm no longer caught up in things that really don't matter." (Linda Benton McCloskey, USA)

- "It's exciting, inspiring—fills my heart and soul. It is what I am meant to be doing. I am grateful for the opportunity to spend the second part of my life making art." (Olga Campbell, Canada)

- "It's not about the end result; it's about the joy of creating. Period." (Judy Shreve, USA)

- "Learning to see differently, to feel immense joy in making art that is mine and that, no one can take away." (Rosa Vera, USA)

- "Being able to create in any way is a true joy and a gift to yourself. Being able to lose yourself in the process is the best therapy ever." (Carol Ludgate, USA)

How wonderful that one of the greatest benefits of coming to art later in life is joy!

In his book *Successful Aging, A Neuroscientist Explores the Power and Potential of Our Lives,* Daniel Levitin states, "When older people look back on their lives and are asked to pinpoint the age at which they were happiest, what do you suppose they say? Not age eight when they had few cares, or during the college years, or the first years of starting a family? The age that comes up most often as the happiest time of one's life is eighty-two!"[7] That is extremely satisfying to me because the age range of the people who responded to my questionnaire was between fifty-six and seventy-nine. This group hasn't even reached their happiest years yet!

Who better to speak of joy than the Dalai Lama and Archbishop Desmond Tutu? In *The Book of Joy: Lasting Happiness in a Changing World,* author Douglas Abrams tells of the lives of these two religious leaders who each experienced incredible suffering and hardship. They came together for a week in 2015 not only to celebrate the Dalai Lama's eightieth birthday but also to provide the inspiration for Abrams to create his book about holding onto joy despite life's inevitable suffering. Their week-long visit was filmed and made into a documentary titled, *Mission of Joy.*

Forced to flee to India to save his life and the lives of Tibetan Buddhist monks, the Dalai Lama was twenty-three years old when the Chinese invaded Tibet in 1959. The Indian government gave them refuge in Dharamsala in northern India and has continued to do so for over fifty years. When Desmond Tutu asked the Dalai Lama how he handles the sadness of being unable to return to his country, the Dalai Lama had a positive framing: he replied that he would not have the freedom to speak and to teach around the world had he remained in Tibet.

Archbishop Desmond Tutu offered his own story of suffering. Born in South Africa in extreme poverty, he became ordained as an Anglican priest and used his position to become an anti-Apartheid and human rights activist. Both leaders have lived through terrifying life-threatening situations and witnessed the suffering of their people. In the book and the film, they looked back on their long lives and discussed the paradox of finding joy in the midst of suffering.

The book was a triumph of joy. We were able to see the childlike silliness these two old friends shared as they teased one another and shared deep laughter. There's a story that Abrams tells about their playful, joyful friendship:

> Once as they were walking on stage to give a talk, the Dalai Lama—the world's icon of compassion and peace—pretended to choke his spiritual brother. The Archbishop turned to the Dalai Lama and said, 'Hey the cameras are on, act like a *holy* man.'[8]

The Archbishop, in a more serious moment, said:

> If we think we want to get joy for ourselves, we must realize that it's very short-sighted, short-lived. Joy is the reward really, of seeking to give joy to others. When you show compassion, when you show caring, when you show love to others, do things for others, in a wonderful way you have a deep joy that you can get in no other way.[9]

Douglas Abrams summed up his experience with these two men:

> The two leaders told us over the course of the week that there is no joy without sorrow, that in fact, it is the pain, the suffering that allows us to experience and appreciate the joy. Indeed the more we turn toward the suffering, our own and others, the more we can turn toward joy. We accept them both, turning the volume of life up, or we turn our backs on life itself, becoming deaf to its music. They

had also told us and demonstrated that true joy is a way of being, not a fleeting emotion. What they had cultivated in their long lives was that enduring trait of joyfulness. They had warned us that we cannot pursue joy as an end in itself, or we will miss the bus. Joy comes, rather, from daily thoughts, feelings, and actions. And they had told us repeatedly the action that gets us on the bus: bringing joy to others.[10]

By the time we're in our older years, we've lived through heartbreaks, grief at the deaths of friends and family, illness, sadness, but also delights, and laughter, and celebrations. While our scales of grief, sorrow, and suffering may not be the same as that experienced by the Dalai Lama or Archbishop Desmond Tutu, we have each carried our own personal suffering. Coming through that suffering to art brings joy.

Chapter 5:
Community

The only thing that really matters in life
are your relationships to other people.
—George E. Valliant

Whether collaborating with a partner to have exhibitions together, as many artists have done, or joining a collective, as Canadian artist Martina Edmonson did, artists who responded to the questionnaire told me that the social aspect of art has been an important benefit for them. They formed whole new communities of friends who share the love of art. When she graduated from art school in Toronto in 2002 as a mature artist, Martina's collective exhibited together on a yearly basis.

Community can be broadly defined as family who help us, other artists we associate with or show with, or for some, it's creating art through community or working with others on a sizable project. Respondents described their connection with community in these ways:

- "A passion for painting is a bridge between people, and I have found most artists to be incredibly generous and kind. I cannot thank enough the experienced artists who gave me a helping hand, generosity and encouragement writ very large. (Maggy Herbert-Johnson, UK)

- [My husband] ""does not create art as such but he advises, encourages, passes on research he's read. He frames the art, packs up art and schleps it off to shows and galleries. I had longed for this kind of working together and it has come into being—a dream come true." (Sue Smith, Canada)

- "I welcome the art openings that bring art lovers together, allow opportunities for education and networking and give one a sense of the artist community." (Genevie Henderson, Canada)

Some artists find community in the way they create their art. In the summer of 2019, I heard ninety-nine-year-old Thelma Pepper, a Saskatchewan photographer, interviewed on CBC radio. She spoke with the energy and the enthusiasm of a much younger woman about her newly published book, titled simply, *Thelma: A Life in Pictures*. Growing up in the small village of Kingston, Nova Scotia, Thelma was inspired by her father's joy in photography and worked alongside him as she learned to develop film in their basement darkroom.

Thelma wrote about being a good student and an avid tennis player. She was awarded a scholarship to Acadia University where she studied botany and then went on to take further studies at McGill University in Montreal. It was there she met and married Jim Pepper, also a botanist. They moved first of all to Guelph, Ontario, settling eventually in Saskatchewan where Jim taught at the University of Saskatchewan in Saskatoon.

While she learned about photography when she was young and always had an interest in taking photographs, it never occurred to her to become a photographer. In fact, it was Thelma's husband, Jim, who took the photographs in the family and while on a visit from Nova Scotia, it was her father who helped install a darkroom in their basement for Jim. Gradually her four children grew up and left home. About that time, Thelma writes, "I spent my whole life not really doing anything for myself, didn't I? And now that life was at the stage when my children left home, I felt I had nothing of my own. I knew I had to find something that made me feel good about myself."[11] She was nearly sixty. Thelma fell into depression.

After her mother's passing, Thelma inherited thousands of her father's photographic negatives. Remembering how happy she'd been in the darkroom with her dad, Thelma decided to print them. She experienced boundless creative energy in this work, losing herself and finding herself. While she was skilled in the darkroom, Thelma needed to find her way with the camera. She began by joining the Saskatoon Camera Club and buying herself an enormously expensive German camera, thereby expressing her independence and starting the self-reliant chapter in her life.

While gradually working on expanding her camera skills, Thelma also did some volunteer work: reading stories to the residents of the nearby seniors' home. As she read them books on pioneer life, the floodgates of their memories opened and Thelma watched as their faces lit up while telling their stories. Naturally, she wanted to take their portraits. Using a tripod and remote cable, she snapped their portraits unobtrusively while they chatted. Thelma learned that she loved making the seniors happy by sharing her photos with them. Slowly, she began recording their stories, learning all she could about them, sometimes inviting them for a drive in the country to visit the places where their stories began. Eventually, Thelma had an exhibition of these intimate, personal photographs.

Delighted to have found her life's passion, even late in life, Thelma advises others to "do something creative, whatever it might be. Believe in yourself, and if that fails, believe the people who believe in you. Find your passion and you'll find yourself. Follow the story lines that uplift you, not defeat you, and therein lies the confidence to face life's challenges with courage and creativity."[12]

Lillian Michiko Blakey, a seventy-six-year-old friend and a Japanese Canadian, is another artist who, like Thelma, has found community through her art practice. Lillian wrote an email to tell me the story of how she researched and shared the story of her Japanese heritage.

During WW II, beginning in early 1942, the Canadian government detained and dispossessed more than 90 percent of Japanese Canadians, some 22,000 people, living in British Columbia. They were detained under the War Measures Act and were relocated for the rest of the War, losing their civil liberties, personal property, buildings, land, communities, and way of life. Some were interned in camps where they were separated from their loved ones. To keep the family together, Lillian's grandparents and their seven children (Lillian's mother was one of them) chose to be sent to a sugar beet farm in Alberta where they were given a filthy chicken coop as their home with no running water or electricity. Freezing in the cold Alberta winter, they had to break the ice off the bucket of water they kept indoors for drinking and washing up. At the end of WW II, many Japanese Canadians were deported to Japan. Lillian's family was separated. Some went to Japan, some stayed in Canada. Other Japanese Canadians were unable to travel for five more years. When they were able to travel, Lillian's family moved to Ontario. Japanese Canadians didn't gather together in communities; they lived apart and many intermarried with non-Japanese, as Lillian did. Lillian felt shame about her family history. Caught between two cultures, she felt neither Japanese nor Canadian.

About a year ago, Lillian contacted Jeff Chiba Stearns, a fourth generation mixed Japanese Canadian filmmaker in British Columbia with the idea of making a film about her grandmother's story that would help Canadian children learn about this treatment of Japanese Canadians. "I had created a book of photos of my grandmother's journey as a picture bride to Canada and all of the challenges she had endured during the War and after." Lillian described picture brides in this way:

> The first immigrants from Japan in the early 1900s were young men sent to North America by their starving families to make their fortune abroad and to send money home.

The only way they could be married to young women in Japan was through a go-between who would arrange the transaction. The go-between would carry a photo of the man in North America to a woman's family. If she liked the way the man looked, the go-between would take her picture back to the man. If they both agreed, they would be married by proxy and she would then travel to meet her husband. These Japanese women became known as "picture brides." In those days, women could not inherit and if she did not find a husband in Japan, she would be left penniless.

Instead of making a film, Jeff had the idea of creating a graphic novel. Lillian writes, "We collaborated and in six months we produced a graphic novel, *On Being Yukiko.*"

While dealing with a very difficult topic, the graphic novel format is appealing and somehow makes the topic is easier to digest. *On Being Yukiko* has been so successful that the first printing sold out in just six months with Lillian and Jeff doing many Zoom presentations. Their goal is to spread the story of the horrendous treatment of Japanese Canadians during WW II as widely as they can. Lillian comments, "It's especially important to have the book in classrooms in order for Canadians to know this shameful part of our history and, most importantly, to understand that this must never happen to Canadian citizens again."[13] Lillian created community through the process of researching and writing the book and, as well, she has more deeply connected with the Japanese community in Canada.

Besides creating community by sharing important life stories through our art, we also share the simple joys of finding like-minded friends. English artist Carol Watson shares:

> Art has changed my life. I have met some lovely people in my teaching. It has been so rewarding opening peoples' eyes to the beauty of the world, nature, colours and

texture. It has kept me active and occupied my mind and hands, which has made me a more interesting person.

American respondent Lynn Alker shares,

> I have made the most amazing friendships with the most interesting people that I now have time to focus on and learn from. Artists are so complex and most have such inspiring backgrounds. I feel as though I'm part of an exclusive club that generates energy, enthusiasm and social change.

These respondents found connection to community through their art, whether exhibiting with other like-minded artists, travelling to workshops, or creating work that involves community. Or, whether, like Lillian Blakey, their work has pushed them to do research into their own family stories, finding through that research, a sense of purpose and connection with others who have similar stories.

Chapter 6:
Travel

We travel because we need to, because distance and difference are the secret tonic to creativity. When we get home, home is still the same. But everything in our mind has changed and that changes everything.
—Jonah Lehrer

The artists who responded to my questionnaire recognized that one of the benefits of coming to art later in life is having the time and opportunity to travel with a community of like-minded people, and go to art workshops or artist residencies. In his essay, *Why We Travel*, Pico Iyer writes:

> We travel, initially, to lose ourselves; and we travel, next, to find ourselves. We travel to open our hearts and eyes and learn more about the world than our newspapers will accommodate... And we travel, in essence, to become young fools again—to slow time down and get taken in, and fall in love once more....
>
> And if travel is like love, it is, in the end, mostly because it's a heightened state of awareness, in which we are

mindful, receptive, undimmed by familiarity and ready to be transformed.[14]

Travelling can actually keep us healthier, reports a joint study from the Global Commission on Aging and Transamerica Center for Retirement Studies, in partnership with the US Travel Association. The study found that women who vacation at least twice a year show a significantly lower risk of suffering a heart attack than those who only travel every six years or so. The same is true for men. Men who do not take an annual vacation show a twenty percent higher risk of death and thirty percent greater risk of heart disease. One study found that people also experience a direct increase in happiness from just planning a trip. The anticipation of taking a vacation is far greater than the anticipation of acquiring a physical possession. Thus, the study indicates that the benefits of traveling abroad begin well before the trip does.[15]

Studies have also shown that travel builds social ties, which nurtures interest in life-long learning. And small groups are especially able to deliver personal interactions, whether enjoying a picnic lunch by a vista, or encounters with local families during home-hosted lunches and dinners. Active travel is proven to lower health risks such as diabetes, metabolic syndrome, high blood pressure, heart disease, colon cancer, breast cancer, depression levels and more, according to the Physical Activity Guidelines Advisory Committee.[16]

Even more important than this are the studies that have shown a correlation between creativity and travel. An article in *The Atlantic* reports that spending time abroad may have the potential to affect mental change. In general, creativity is related to neuroplasticity, or how the brain is wired. Neural pathways are influenced by environment and habit, meaning they're also sensitive to change: New sounds, smells, languages, tastes, sensations, and sights spark different synapses in the brain and may have the potential to revitalize the mind.[17]

I've always loved to travel, especially to wild and remote places, gathering ideas and inspiration for my paintings. Over the last few years, for example, I visited several stone circles in isolated locations in Scotland and Ireland as well as igloo-shaped passage graves. While their purpose in some cases is unclear, many of these ancient stone sites are oriented toward a certain position of the sun or moon in the sky over the course of a year, whether the rising sun at winter solstice, autumnal equinox, or the way the moon appears to stand still in the sky in an eighteen-year cycle. While visiting these sites, I had the idea that I was, in a sense, gathering light to bring home and share in my paintings. I called the long series of paintings I created from that idea, Gathering Light.

My world expands and I gather inspiration when I travel, but living on an artist's unsteady salary, I've had to be creative in finding inexpensive ways to travel. Several years ago, I discovered artist residencies, which provide accommodation and small studio spaces. These residencies are available to artists all over the world. Some are free depending on acceptance of your application, while others cost a small amount. I prefer ones that are remote but provide accommodation to a small group of artists rather than just one person. The interaction with artists from other countries is a stimulating, enlightening, and enriching experience.

Fifteen years ago, I had the idea to combine my love of travel with my love of teaching painting and I began to offer workshops in various parts of Canada, the US, as well as in Sweden and Iceland. Over time, this evolved into the Workshops in Wild Places project, in which I organize and lead small groups of artists to paint in various remote, awe-inspiring locations in the world three or four times per year. For example, I've recently led painting trips to the ancient caravan route in Morocco; to the rugged Burren in Ireland; to a small and remote island off the north tip of Newfoundland to see whales and icebergs; to a retreat centre on the Camino in Spain to make paint from earth pigments; and to the far west coast of Canada to see storms come in across the Pacific.

A key aspect of all of these workshops is helping artists deepen their personal relationship with nature. We're all disconnected from nature. I believe that's why the Earth is in such crisis. It is my hope that through these travel workshops, artists will deepen their connection and recognize their oneness with the Earth, to reconnect with a sense of wonder, perhaps that joy, that love would be passed on to their students and their audiences, especially if they speak about it in their artist talks and write about it in their artist statements. To me, this is one of the wonderful potential gifts of travel.

Travelling with other artistic souls, painting together, eating communal meals, and staying in the same accommodation builds camaraderie, which is nurturing and important. We share a sense of community, the understanding of the creative process, the way we see things, and a connection with place. We're not all the same and there can be differences and misunderstandings, but there's a way of seeing the world that is similar—a cross-pollination of ideas, an understanding of what each other is aiming to do, an easy sense of community, and a deepening love of the Earth.

Chapter 7:
Healing

The act of making art is both scary and healing.
Art brings light to places that have remained dark.
Art brings perspective. Making art, at any level,
is an act of courage and an expression of faith.
—Julia Cameron

Art has long been known as a practice that has health benefits for practitioners, whatever their age or skill level. In a recent study published in the *Journal of the American Art Therapy Association,* investigators looked at the impact of visual art making on the cortisol levels of thirty-nine healthy adults. Participants provided saliva samples to assess the level of cortisol (the body's main stress hormone) before and after forty-five minutes of art making. Participants also provided written responses about the experience at the end of the session. Results indicate that art making resulted in statistically significant lowering of cortisol levels. Participants' written responses indicated that they found the art making session to be relaxing, enjoyable, and helpful for learning about new aspects of self, freeing from constraints, a process involving struggling to create something and then losing themselves in the work. One doesn't have to be a talented artist to enjoy the health benefits of art.[18]

While creating art can lower cortisol levels, there is evidence of an even more profound effect too. Some of the artists who responded to my questionnaire, when asked what brought them to art, told of the deep healing that occurred through art when recovering from physical or emotional trauma or abuse.

For abstract painter Audrey Phillips from the US, creating art was a spontaneous reaction to grief. Her story was documented in *AARP Magazine*. The article is published here with Audrey's permission.

> One morning in 1989, Phillips got a phone call at work from her father in Panama Beach, Florida. He was 'just checking in,' he claimed. But Phillips, then 33 years old and a recently divorced marketing executive at the Orlando Sentinel, sensed something was amiss; normally the voice checking in was that of her mother, Lola Mae. That afternoon, her father called again. 'We've got a problem,' he told Phillips, 'Mom hasn't been home since yesterday.' Two days after she went missing, Lola Mae's body was discovered in a secluded wood near the Alabama border. She and an employee in her consignment shop had been abducted and murdered in a botched robbery. (Their 22-year-old killer is now serving back-to-back life sentences.) Traumatized, Phillips began a decade-long slide whose casualties included her job and her faith. She got married again, but divorced. She turned to therapy and yoga in a bid to salve the pain and quell the rage.
>
> In 2000, Phillips was visiting a close friend in New Mexico who happened to be an artist. Aware that Phillips had studied graphic design before she went into marketing, the friend bought her some paper and pastels and urged her to try some drawings. Abruptly the pictures tumbled forth. The subject: the killer's face—one version after another in wild, furious, almost brutal renditions. "I'd been thinking

about it a long time," Phillips reflects. "And it came out with such energy—I probably had 30 pieces of art when I was done. I was like, 'Thank God that's out on the page and not inside me anymore.'" Day after day for the next several years, Phillips patiently refined her technique, sometimes standing entranced before her easel for hours. Today, she is an award-winning abstract artist and teacher who works in acrylic and encaustic in her home studio in Florida. "Painting catapulted me through my final phase of grieving and loss, she reflects. It basically saved my life."[19]

Art basically saved Canadian respondent Rex Duff's life too. He seemed driven to share his story with me. I was a juror for an art show in Winnipeg, Manitoba and mentioned in a talk I gave afterwards that I was writing a book. I invited them to share their stories with me. While Rex didn't come to art later in life, the directness of his story and the fact that art played such a profoundly healing and steady role in his life, compelled me to share it. Rex's parents went through a divorce when he was very young and, for some reason he doesn't understand, they put Rex in a foster home. He shared his traumatizing experiences:

> By the time I was 10, due to having been in several abusive foster homes, I ended up in a home for disturbed children where I received the first gift I can remember: a paint by number set. When the painting was finished there was still paint left over. One night the 'night mother' caught me sitting by the window making a painting of trees that were lit by the street light. The next night she gave me a box of oil paints and a couple of canvas boards and then on the weekends we would go painting outdoors... After leaving the home, I was in a private religious school where I was asked to do the backdrop for the girl's precision swim team, which consisted of the island Bali Hai from the movie 'South Pacific'.

Art has always been a stable force in Rex's life, something he comes back to time and time again:

> After graduation I joined the Air Force and was not able to paint in the barracks due to the fire hazard and odors. Marriage and two young children also curtailed painting because of the hazards. I had an accident at work and was unemployed for a year during which time I enrolled in a correspondence course with Famous Artists School. For the next few years I painted sporadically and took classes at the Winnipeg Art Gallery. I moved to Toronto and started a renovation company which left no time for outside interests. In 2016 my health declined to such an extent that I had to stop the reno business and, after regaining some of my health, I began painting again. Now painting is a way of keeping me from dwelling on my health problems.

While Rex Duff tells how art helped him cope with the emotional trauma of abusive foster homes, American respondent, Lisa Boardwine's story, highlights the role art played in her healing from the physical trauma caused by a car accident. Lisa tells first of some of the difficulties in promoting her art. Coming from a small town caused her to have to travel for many years doing outdoor shows and festivals. After a show one day, Lisa and a friend were walking through a parking lot, going to their cars and the accident happened:

> All of a sudden, we heard loud acceleration coming straight towards us! There was no time to run, move out of the way or save ourselves from being hit. In a split second, the vehicle slammed into a parked car, which hit us and trapped us between the car and a building. My right foot was crushed and my left shoulder broken... During that time of healing, my days were filled with much soul search-ing of how this would impact my life and my art. Even

though I was not able to paint for a long period of time, I would go to my studio. The studio became a sanctuary for me. Just to sit in my creative space (in a wheelchair) was good medicine! I felt a part of the world again! I was in a wheelchair for many months. For the first 4-5 months they thought they might have to amputate my foot. With my opposite shoulder broken in three places, I could not use a walker or crutches, or even roll myself in a wheelchair to get to my studio. When I started to heal and the scare was over about losing my foot, I would get my mom or my husband to take me to my studio. Art truly saved me. It was my driving passion to be in the studio making art and expressing myself in paint. I began by listening to music, doing meditative thoughtfulness and prayer; then I started putting things in folders, looking through art books and photos, playing with art materials and different papers, and then I started holding a sketchpad in my lap to make marks! I had a friend arrange a palette on a side table, so I could paint on my lap. Gradually with time, I progressed to standing at my easel to paint. It was like discovering art a second time in my life. The joy of creating and the passion for the process seemed more precious and somehow new with a different focus. I embraced this time to experiment, explore, and express the work I had always held in my heart.

A Canadian respondent, who wishes to be referred to as Adriana, is an artist who participated in one of my workshops. In her response to my questionnaire, she wrote how art helped her heal from an abusive childhood. Because I knew her slightly, I wrote to ask if she'd elaborate on her story. While it deals with the extremely disturbing aspect of parental sexual abuse, Adriana wanted to share it here. Through years of therapy, and with the help of a very supportive husband, she was able to heal. Her art practice was a powerful ally on this journey. Here is Adriana's story in her own words, and with her permission:

> I was the youngest of nine children. I survived childhood trauma, which occurred within the family, as well as with organized abuse outside of the family. To survive that which was intolerable, I fragmented and developed a dissociative disorder. In essence the fragmentation saved me. I carried few memories of my childhood into my teenage and early adult years. One clear memory was from a very young age looking out at the world in wonderment and awe. And then, as if an eclipse occurred, there was a shift in how I experienced life. I looked outward with great apprehension and fear. It would take years before I could name what had happened, though I knew instinctively I had lost a sense of belonging.
>
> At the age of seventeen I became suicidal. I was fortunate in having the unfaltering support of my partner, who would later become my husband. I asked him in countless ways for reassurance and I struggled to feel safe within my own self and the world. Later in life I would recognize the need to reclaim a trust within and in life generally. I was deeply afraid of catastrophic events and could not connect to the reason for my terror as I had dissociated from the atrocities of abuse that had happened. Somehow I survived the years of transitioning into adulthood.
>
> My past went underground until my first child was born… At three months of age my son needed surgery for pyloric stenosis, a condition in which the baby's pylorus muscle, which connects the stomach and the small intestine, swells and thickens causing food to be blocked.

The pediatrician spoke to me in the hallway following surgery and said, 'Years ago a baby would die with the condition.' I had no response, though was flooded with senseless guilt and a renewed fear for my son's safety in the world. I began to question whether I could keep him safe and there was a growing instability in my confidence as a young mother. My son was hospitalized eight times in his first year.

I lost sight of the difference between day and night. I stayed in the hospital each time my son was admitted. It was then, when I was utterly exhausted and concerned for my son's health, that the unresolved trauma of the past began to seep through. Everywhere I looked I saw danger. I was on constant and vigilant watch. Any sense of safety I had in the world and deep within my own self had shattered.

When the long journey of recovery from trauma began, the body remembered first. The sensations of the trauma on my body would last seconds, rise to the surface, and then recede. They would reoccur throughout the day, taking as long as needed for acceptance to take hold, and for the memories to become conscious. In the beginning when I could not stay with what my body was telling me, the sensations would persist in intensity. Among them was a memory, which still revisits when there is significant stress, of being hit on the face. When the sensations first started many years earlier, I would drop whatever I was doing in the moment and run to the bathroom mirror, expecting bruises to appear on my face.

I was in my thirties when I started to paint in between the tumultuous work of connecting the present day fears to the trauma of the past. There was a growing awareness as the memories surfaced and associated directly to the fears that overshadowed my life. I painted horses, sea otters, and wild gardens on driftwood and on old clay pots.

When my sons were in school and on the days I felt well enough, I walked the beaches, collecting driftwood that piled at the back door. Recovering from the trauma and living with the impact of its residue in my daily life was often overwhelming. When I turned to painting, I discovered my mind would calm and there was a meditative quality in the act of creating. During the most difficult periods of healing, I journaled what needed to be expressed with rudimentary printing and large loop writing. When words would fail me I would draw stick people that illustrated memories in pictures—visceral in their connection to the trauma.

Throughout the years I read stories of others who had survived and thrived in the aftermath of trauma. In their voices I found validation and a strength of spirit that carried me through many of my darkest times. I struggled to put my recovery into words. It was when I was working with a therapist who had significant experience in childhood trauma recovery, and specifically dissociate disorders, that I began to write. This was the start of a deeper integration of the split off parts of the self. I would come to realize the potential of how creativity, whether writing or painting, helped free the hold of trauma.

Finding my voice in writing, and what I would find in painting in the years to come, brought the challenge of stepping aside and allowing the work to flow through. I took writing courses over a period of five years. In 2012,

I had an excerpt of my recovery journey published in 'Healing the Unimaginable: Treating Ritual Abuse and Mind Control' written by Alison Miller, my therapist at the time. In 2014, I also had an excerpt published in 'Becoming Yourself: Overcoming Mind Control and Ritual Abuse' also written by Alison Miller. For both publications, I wrote in the style of memoir and in present tense. My writing traced back over the trauma and brought about a greater awareness of its far-reaching hurt and impact on how I moved through the world.

Although writing was powerful in its own right and held a significant role in healing alongside therapy, it also prompted reliving the traumatic experiences. I also came to realize that there was a limit to my ability to fully communicate the devastating impact of the trauma. Often I could not find the words to articulate what had happened in the formative years; the trauma experienced by many of the younger fragmented parts of me could not be translated into verbal expression.

Following the publication of my last writing piece I yearned for solitude. Still there was the strong pull to continue the journey of healing. I knew from previous years that I needed to create in a meaningful way. There had been periods of time when I did not write or paint, and I would become depressed and pulled into isolation. Painting provided the fragmented parts a 'voice' in the world in a different way than writing. It held the potential power to remove the barriers between the fragmented parts, and allowed the expression of emotions that were complex and implicitly woven into my being. Over the years their place of being seen was primarily limited to therapy sessions. I would often remain in the background while the focus of therapy was on the fragmented parts of me, bringing to light the long held hurt of the past. Therapy provided the needed support to encourage integration. With my last therapist I felt supported and understood. I learned how to contain memories that would overwhelm me. Though when I was on my own I had difficulty relating to the fragmented parts of me. Painting and giving space for self-expression helped anchor me to the present. Creativity, without conscious effort, would allow wounded parts to participate in creativity, helping to recover a sense of belonging to the wholeness of being.

Returning to painting was a natural redirection from writing. The act of creating art helped me move from mind to heart, and to the core of my feelings. In the midst of painting I would find myself crying with the release of grief which had always been difficult to express otherwise. There were emotions that overlapped that I could not name, though I acknowledged their existence. I would go inward and access a pathway for the fragmentation to unify and be expressed visually. I felt safe in my creative space. There was no threat to my safety, or the need to remain hidden. There was an opening to the silent space inside, and therein I began to experience the healing of my spirituality. The expression was often subtle and over time, in addition to therapy, I felt a greater healing take place.

In more recent years my painting has evolved more intuitively, with the outcome being primarily abstract landscape. Throughout the years I found healing and a nurturance for creativity in nature. My hope is to learn to let go further and develop a greater transparency in my creative endeavours as they relate to continued healing.

In recent years I have developed a love for oil and cold wax. Through this medium I discovered the potential to create visual depth, history, and layers of self-expression. My explorations continue to evolve towards a greater sense of wholeness. The healing that painting brings forth expanded beyond time spent in the studio. It has and continues to graciously enhance the aliveness of simply being and the awe and wonder of interconnectedness in life itself.

These four powerful stories show the healing power art can have in our lives, how it can nurture our souls, and may help us withstand deep physical pain and emotional trauma.

Chapter 8:
Continuing to Grow

Happiness is neither virtue nor pleasure nor this thing nor that but simply growth. We are happy when we are growing.
—W.B. Yeats

When I was a first-year student at university, I routinely chose a seat about half-way back in the large classroom theatres. Being very shy and unsure of myself, I wanted a safe spot where I could avoid eye contact with the professors. I noticed that the handful of middle-aged students (all women) in attendance chose the same spot each time as well: the very front row. They asked the professors all kinds of things, everything from simple queries to the thoughtful kinds of questions that showed how much preparation they had done. Very few of us younger students had the courage to ask a question for fear of embarrassing ourselves, and we weren't nearly as prepared. On the other hand, those women seemed to care nothing about being embarrassed. I was impressed with their fearlessness, their confidence.

About three decades later, as a middle-aged woman, I enrolled at the Ontario College of Art & Design in Toronto. Just like the older women my younger self had encountered at university, I found myself sitting in the front row of every art history class asking every question that entered my head. I was hungry to learn. While I was terrified of not being good enough at my chosen subjects—drawing and painting—I was fearless when it came to asking questions. Sensing my lack of self-consciousness, the younger students would sometimes tap me on the shoulder to ask me to put forward a question they were too shy to ask. It made me realize how much confidence and maturity I had gained over those intervening years.

I was an eager student of art history, and I was over-prepared for my class projects and assignments. My presentations were too long and too comprehensive for what the teachers expected. There seemed to be so much to learn, I hardly knew when to stop, unlike in my earlier university days where I seemed to know *exactly* what it took to get a respectable B.

Nowadays, I find that most of the students in the painting workshops I teach who have come to art later in their lives, just as I did, are also eager to learn. Many are retired or semi-retired and have achieved a level of skill and success in their careers. For those who have a pension, the pressure to make money as artists is alleviated. Most artists hope to sell their work at some point, as much for affirmation as for remuneration. There is a tendency to think that if a painting sells, it must be good. But creating paintings just for the purpose of making money can be stifling. It's important for older students to realize that one of the big gifts they bring, if they have some sort of pension, is the freedom to do whatever they want. If they aren't dependent on art sales for income, they have great liberty to explore and learn and discover the creative side of themselves.

One artist who came to art very late in life is Frieda Lefeber, who began painting at age seventy-six. I read about her on social media and then did some research to learn more about her. According to an article in *The Philadelphia Inquirer,* Lefeber turned 100 in March 2015 and celebrated with her first solo art exhibition, a retrospective of landscape and portrait paintings that opened at a Philadelphia gallery.[20] A mother, grandmother, retired nurse, and Holocaust survivor, Lefeber studied at the Pennsylvania Academy of Fine Arts, earning her certificate from there when she was eighty-three.

The seeds of Lefeber's career as an artist were planted many years earlier when someone saw a painting she had done and told her that she had talent. "I didn't know that I had any talent," she claimed in the article. That comment was encouragement enough, and she soon started at the Arts Academy. After graduating from there, Lefeber made regular trips to Germany, Italy, and France, taking art classes with teachers who inspired her. Her preference was plein air landscape painting, done in an impressionistic style. She painted regularly until she was one hundred but not with the same intensity as when she was in her seventies. She died in 2018 at one hundred three.

There's a wealth of learning and life that feeds into the art of older folks. A few years ago, there was a woman in one of my abstract painting workshops named Dorothy, aged ninety-two. She came into class on a walker. Dorothy had been a successful ceramicist for decades, making wildly creative sculptural pieces. But as her strength slowly diminished over the years, she gave up pottery and took up printmaking and then painting. For her entire life, Dorothy maintained a playful attitude, which was on display in my class. I noticed that her work was exploratory, loose, and free, similar in feeling to her ceramic sculptures. She wasn't interested in being perfect or making a product, she was there for the sheer enjoyment of making art, the sheer enjoyment of learning and playing and growing.

I'm inspired by older women who are curious and adventurous, and I love reading their stories. In her beautiful book *The Paper Garden: An Artist Begins Her Life Work at 72*, renowned poet Molly Peacock tells the riveting history of Mary Delany (1700-1788), who became a skilled botanical collage artist late in life. Perhaps the unique thing about English-born Delany was that she began her famous body of work in her seventies. An aristocrat, she survived personal trials including a teenage marriage to a man her grandfather's age and the loss of a beloved second husband. Music, embroidery, sketching, and cutting out silhouettes were the pastimes available to women in Mrs. Delany's day, and they enabled her to overcome her life challenges and to survive. She was also an avid botanist who corresponded with some of the great minds of her age. By the time she was in her seventies, Mrs. Delany put all of these skills and life experiences into creating a vast collection of floral collages, a brand-new art form at the time. In the span of ten years, she created 985 botanically correct cut-paper flowers that are now in the collection of the British Museum.

"Mary Delany's story is one of a woman who overcame the many obstacles thrown in her path. She never perceived her life as going in a straight line toward something."[21] While some thought it was a shame Mrs. Delany was married to that "old coot," as otherwise, she would have done the brilliant collages earlier, Peacock disagrees: "I don't actually think so. Some things in life take living long enough to create."[22]

Artist True Ryndes, a questionnaire respondent from the US, has indicated something similar about coming to art later in life:

> Painting at this stage of my life has provided me a vehicle for focus, mental agility and excitement once I retired…
> I would not be good at golf or cards, though many people are. I would not be happy watching TV and the aquarium, as my dad did when he retired. That really sounds like Retirement, an exhaling and withdrawing from the public arena. The word that better captures my sense of this period would be 'inspirement,' a continued breathing in, waking up curious about the lessons, not the score.

Like Ryndes, I find myself continually curious about the lessons art teaches us, and, like Mary Delany, I've discovered an ability to synthesize my different experiences drawn from over seven decades of living. I've become more introspective, interested in how the various parts of my life and work interconnect. Continuing to grow is an important benefit of coming to art later in life.

Part III
Coming to Art
Later in Life:
Challenges

Chapter 9:
Self Doubt

Because in the end, you won't remember the time
you spent working in the office or mowing your lawn.
Climb that goddamn mountain.
—Jack Kerouac

The biggest challenge older artists reported, by far, was self-doubt. On the one hand, older artists have much more self-confidence gained from dealing with life, knowing that they are good at problem -solving, which they've had to do throughout their lives. When it comes to learning something new, though, breaking through the boundaries of their current lives, opening up to new possibilities and learning new skills, they find the biggest challenge is self-doubt.

Maybe self-doubt is like shyness. As I mentioned, I was shy when I was a young woman and as I got older I realized that I may have been focusing too much on myself, instead of looking outward toward others. That realization was life-changing. I threw off the shyness almost overnight to focus on others. Isn't self-doubt like that—focusing too much on the self? These respondents, however, didn't stop their pursuit of becoming artists because of self-doubt. They continued anyway, until they overcame that obstacle:

- "The biggest challenge by far, was my own insecurity and lack of self-confidence." (James Edward Scherbarth, USA)

- "I had to do my own personal growth work to become more assertive and self-confident." (Jill Segal, Canada)

- "The story about my early experience [of her kindergarten teacher painfully belittling her work in class], stayed with me a long time because I told myself over the years that I couldn't make art." (Geri de Gruy, USA)

What makes a person risk coming to art at an older age, especially if like Geri, they had such humiliating experiences with art as children or, like Canadian respondent Michela Sorrentino, who as a young woman was belittled in art college? What is it about art that drives us go deep into our souls to connect with the mystery that is there, pushing through our self-doubts and fears?

In the newsletter, *Brain Pickings*, (now called the Marginalian), Amanda Palmer writes about overcoming self-doubt through the difficult experience of watching her best friend die:

> Everyone in this room is going to be gone pretty quickly—and we will have either made something or not made something. The artists that inspire me are the ones that I look at and go, 'Oh my god—you didn't have to go there. It would've been safer not to—but, for whatever reason, you did.' And every time death happens, I'm reminded that it's stupid to be safe... Usually, whatever that is—wherever you don't want to go, whatever that risk is, wherever the unsafe place is—that really is the gift that you have to give.[23]

Van Gogh, an expert in self-doubt, writes in his letter to his brother Theo on October 2, 1884,

If one wants to be active, one mustn't be afraid to do something wrong sometimes, not afraid to lapse into some mistakes. To be good—many people think that they'll achieve it by *doing no harm*—and that's a lie… That leads to stagnation, to mediocrity. *Just slap something on it* when you see a blank canvas staring at you with a sort of imbecility…Many painters *are afraid* of the blank *canvas*, but the blank canvas *is afraid* of the truly passionate painter who dares—and who has once broken the spell of 'you can't.' [24]

Kathy Stinson is a hugely successful, multiple award-winning Canadian author of children's books. Among them are *Red is Best*, *The Dog Who Wanted to Fly*, and *The Man with the Violin*. Before she began writing children's books, Kathy was home with her kids reading books to them night after night and she kept thinking, 'Maybe someday I'll write, maybe someday I'll write'. And then finally, she said to herself, 'OK, if maybe someday, what's wrong with today?'.

Kathy recently felt a call to move in another direction in her writing, but was uncertain. Tucking her well-used journal of notes that she calls 'Scribblings" into her suitcase, she booked a retreat for a week at a B&B in a nearby city to give herself some uninterrupted time of contemplation. There, she looked over old notes she'd written—ideas, thoughts, poems, sketches —looking for threads of connection to point the way. On her return, she wrote a wonderful blog post, entitled "How 7 nudges led me to my new project for the New Year." In it she connected the threads from her scribblings along with things she read or came across serendipitously in the previous month, which she felt were clear signs encouraging her move into poetry. I asked Kathy if she felt it was courageous to change directions at that point in her career. She wrote back:

Yes, there is a risk to it but there's also as much risk in not trying things, getting down the road and asking, 'Why didn't I try? I'll never know if I could have, and now it's too late. I'm afraid to do this (change directions). Maybe I'll find out I can't do it. And maybe I can't. But so?...' In a way it's not different from what I've done before. It feels like a change in direction because if I find it's a good idea and I start feeling capable of it, it could take quite a bit of time… In a way it's like what I've always done. First of all, I tried picture books, then I tried chapter books and then I tried Young Adult books and then short stories and this is one more.

This recent inner urge that led her to take a week sabbatical, has pushed her into exploring writing poetry. She wonders if she can do that and confesses that, "it feels very fragile right now. There's so much I don't know about writing poetry. But that's okay."[25] Kathy's comments echo the sentiments made by Mark Rothko and Adolph Gottlieb, "Art is an adventure into an unknown world, which can be explored only by those willing to take risks."

We all feel fragile when we move in a new direction and that's the beauty of it. Buddhists call it Beginner's Mind. Our work becomes new again. We step with uncertainty. There's a raw honesty about it. Art opens us up, shows us our courage, our perseverance, our strength. It gives us confidence in the midst of fear and self-doubt. It connects us with our core, the golden thread that connects us to our life purpose, the divine within us. We don't walk away the same as we were when we began.

Chapter 10:
Making Space and Time for Art

My responsibility is not to the ordinary, or the timely. My loyalty is to the inner vision, whenever and howsoever it may arrive. If I have a meeting with you at three o'clock, rejoice if I am late. Rejoice even more if I do not arrive at all.
—Mary Oliver

Creating physical space in which to make art is a form of commitment to the work. It's telling the universe that this is important work, even though, initially, we may feel like imposters. In our uncertainty about taking the leap into the art that is calling us, most of us approach it cautiously, on the one hand needing a dedicated space in which to work and on the other hand not willing to allow ourselves that dedicated space to work until we prove to ourselves that we are artists. But wait, how can we become artists without a dedicated space to work?

A friend of mine, whose husband died three years ago, lives alone now in a rambling country house. As she's starting out on her artistic path, she needs to dedicate a space for painting. As a long-time artist, I see so much potential for studio spaces in her home. Her living room, completely unused now, is spacious with a wonderful view over the balsam and spruce forest covering the valley below. She watches movies, reads, and visits with friends in a small and cozy library off the kitchen. Instead of using the huge living room space and converting it into a studio, she has given herself the tiny but light-filled potting room off the garage where her husband used to grow geraniums. It's difficult to allow ourselves to repurpose existing rooms for our art even while living alone in a big house. Of course it's a matter of taking ourselves seriously. And why not? What if we tried out a new space for a year and then lost interest? We could move out the tables and easels and art supplies, lift up the protective coverings on the floor and move the carpets back in place. Nothing would be lost.

As I indicated earlier, when I first began to paint, I painted with watercolour on the kitchen counter between family meal times. Eventually I graduated to the kitchen table, then to the tiny guest bedroom upstairs. No one criticized me for this or even commented on it. I was the one who had been holding myself back. I moved after that, and in the new house I had a separate area in an open family room for a studio. It was a small area and way too open. I could only work there in the daytime on weekdays when no one was home. Even though I'd been painting for about eight years by then, I was still not truly taking myself seriously. Years later, I moved to the country and had a house built, which includes an 800 square feet. studio, large enough for me to teach classes.

James Edward Scherbarth used a corner of his furnace room when he began to paint, doing the same thing I did, gradually allowing himself larger and larger spaces, finally renting a studio space in a building with other artists. Respondent Michela Sorrentino writes about the importance of having a space for art. "I had to make room for my art practice. Without having made the space for my work and making it a priority it would never have taken off."

Art is a long journey. Making a commitment to it can feel like deciding whom to marry. Scary. But we don't have to decide all at once. We can take it slowly, let our feelings guide the way, which is exactly what American novelist E. L. Doctorow implies in his famous quotation, "Writing is like driving at night in the fog. You can only see as far as your headlights, but you can make the whole trip that way."[2] The same applies to painting or any creative endeavour. I didn't realize I'd made a commitment to art until I started calling myself an artist, until I had a studio space in my house, until I started having regular studio hours. One step at a time. Driving in the fog.

Besides finding a dedicated studio space in our homes or elsewhere, there is also the issue of making a commitment of time. Many of the artists who responded indicated that they tried to work at their art when they were younger but found that between caring for children and working at jobs outside the house, finding time for themselves to pursue their art was a huge challenge. It's especially difficult if we're just starting out at art and are unsure of ourselves anyway.

Many artists mentioned the need for self-discipline in time management. "It was a fine balance," writes Michela Sorrentino, "making sure that my family was loved and cared for but that I still had time to myself in order to pursue my art." Canadian respondent Susan Lindsay expresses a similar sentiment. "Life was busy. Raising three kids, balancing the demands of work and family life. I didn't have a lot of spare time."

I came to know Canadian respondent Annie Abdalla through social media when I was heading off to an artist residency in Iceland in 2016. She had been there a few years earlier. We exchanged emails many times over the intervening years. I write about Annie more in another chapter because I'm inspired by her daily dedication to her art. She is on the leadership team at Gampo Abbey, a Tibetan Buddhist monastery in Nova Scotia, Canada. With a rigid monastic schedule to adhere to, Annie keeps breakfast short so she'll have 25 minutes to work on her art back in her room or outside in good weather. She comments, "I'm a big supporter of little bits of effort repeated regularly. Kind of like meditation—it doesn't have to be long every day but even a small daily, or almost daily practise, has an impact." What Annie discovered is what so many artists have discovered: becoming an artist requires dedication and commitment—the commitment of time as well as a dedicated space to work in.

Chapter 11:
Changing Identity

If what you are following is your own true adventure, if it
is something appropriate to your deep spiritual need or
readiness, then magical guides will appear to help you.
If you are ready for it, then doors will open where there
were no doors before, and where there would not be doors
for anyone else. And you must have courage. It's the call to
adventure, which means there is no security, no rules.
—Joseph Campbell

It takes courage to come to art at any age, and it takes *greater* courage
to do it later in life. We have to be willing to be novices again, students.
We have to be strong in the face of discouragement from friends and
loved ones who might not want us to change, and we have to resist
societal pressures that would keep us in a box labeled, 'senior citizen'
or 'retired person.' It takes courage to establish new routines to allow
for this new love in our lives and great strength to show our work in
exhibitions. Mary Oliver, in her poem *The Journey,* writes about the
transformation that happens when, late in life, we finally find what we
were brought here to do: "One day you finally knew what you had to
do, and began, though the voices around you kept shouting their bad
advice—though the whole house began to tremble."[27]

Many of the artists who responded to my questionnaire write that transformation, the changing of their identities, was a big challenge for them. True Ryndes writes:

> Making the transition from being well-known within a professional community to being an unknown person in a community I hadn't helped create was a big challenge. It took me at least a year to 'recalibrate' after leaving hospice [True's work at the time] and get clear about what it mean to have a NEW chapter, not just recycle my old skills in a different way.

James Edward Scherbarth, wrote, "I had to overcome all sorts of inner self-imposed limitations. Also I had the challenge of convincing my family and friends that I needed studio time. I felt I was not being taken seriously". American respondent Gail Baar echoes that last sentiment: "When you are older, it is hard to start something that is new to you, to do something different...hard to make people realize that you are doing it like a career, not as a hobby."

I had similar issues in my own journey to become an artist. My friends acted as though I'd retired and that I'd be available any time of day. I'd only taken my first art class two years previously, so it was no wonder they didn't understand this abrupt change in direction and my effort to start a new career. They kept calling me to chat, to have lunch, to go for walks, or to help out with a volunteer project. They thought painting was just a hobby, a therapy, something to fill my time rather than a job or a calling. Of course, people reflect back to us what we're feeling and what we need to learn, and at that time I was feeling insecure and vulnerable in pursuing what felt like a crazy idea to redefine myself as an artist, especially after only a few short painting classes. I began writing down strict schedules for myself as I tried to fit into the role of an artist, giving myself specific times to paint, to eat lunch, to exercise. I even programmed my answering machine (this was, don't forget, several years ago), to say that I'd be able to return calls only after 4 p.m. I was desperately trying to create open space around me. Creative space.

Many of the people I've taught in my workshops and many of the respondents to my questionnaire have changed careers several times in their lives. I love hearing their stories. One woman worked as a Vaudeville dancer in the Yukon, then a mining camp cook and baker. Another has worked as a ski instructor, an executive search consultant, a fundraiser, an executive director of a non-profit and an art professor. Changing identity to become an artist though seems different, perhaps because there is a misunderstanding that art isn't a real job. It can take a long time of learning and commitment before any paintings will sell, and so, in our commercial world where money is a marker of success, becoming an artist isn't taken seriously.

Even though it's difficult to redefine ourselves after friends and family have seen us in certain roles for many years, changing identity to become an artist can be the most exciting of all career changes. American respondent Carol Retch-Bogart shares:

> I've developed an appreciation and wonderment of what
> is possible to create. I have long marveled at the creations
> of other artists, but to look at a piece of my own creation
> on the wall of a gallery is still mind-boggling.

It's finally having the time to discover ourselves—to see what we like, to learn about what excites us, to go into our souls to connect to our deepest selves.

Chapter 12:
Finding Our Artistic Voices

We create ourselves by our choices.
—Kirkegaard

Whether we know it or not, when we embark on the journey of becoming an artist, we open up. We have to. It's part of the process. And it's in that process that we create ourselves. The artist's voice is a mixture of style, technique, and the message we wish to impart. But that voice can change.

Many years ago I made the choice to become a painter. Or maybe painting chose me. It took time, though, to call myself an artist. First I chose to work in watercolour, then later, in oils. I painted landscapes and still life at first, moving much later into dark and mysterious paintings of vessels. Choice. Choice. Choice. I continued to make choices about my subject matter, and as I grew as an artist and as a person, my work continued to change. Eventually, as I've indicated, I moved into abstraction, where I had endless choice and had to learn to put limitations on my subject matter. I had to make decisions.

There is an underlying connection within our various bodies of work that asserts, 'This is me. This is who I am.' This doesn't mean that each body of work has to have the same colours or lines or shapes, but there will be a thread, a signature ambient sense that runs through all of our work. It doesn't mean we have to choose one topic and paint that endlessly for the rest of our lives. But what is of major importance is to make one body of work at a time—to follow an idea through until it stops asserting itself and we want to stop or pause for a while. Within that body of work the number of paintings produced can vary from thirty to one hundred or more paintings.

So, there is no one voice or artistic style we can have. The work of Anna Maria Maiolino is an excellent example of this. I saw an exhibition of Maiolino's work at the Tapies Museum in Barcelona. Hers were complex works, developed through a variety of media: poetry, woodcuts, photography, film, performance, sculpture. The common thread among the various works and media was her body, her body's relationship with the media. In her artist statement on the wall of the gallery, she described herself as the rhizome. Rhizomes are simply fleshy underground stems. They grow underground or right at ground level with many growing points or eyes similar to potatoes. Poplar trees are rhizomatous.

She explained that her various works came from that rhizome. Had I only seen each body of work separately, I'm not sure I could have seen the connection between them. But when viewed together, there was a link, some sort of sensibility, an idea, a way of handling materials that was particular to Maiolino.

This evidence of an artist's signature coming through a body of work was also evident in a video I came across of the artist Jim Dine in which he is speaking about his retrospective at Pace Wildenstein Gallery in 2009.[28] I have always loved his intense and wide-ranging creativity. One of the main objectives in his art practice, he said, is to explore his own unconscious. He intuitively goes wherever his intuition takes him, whether making sculptures of his childhood love, Pinocchio; writing poetry on walls and objects and then photographing that; or drawing self-portraits on museum walls and then washing them away at the end of the exhibit. There is a thread, a link that runs through his work—the intense energy of the work, the nervous line he makes, and the odd, dream-like nature of the images he repeats in his drawings and sculptures. It's a quality that is hard to define, maybe the essence of him as a person.

Our personal voice is with us all along. It's who we are. We can't escape it. That doesn't mean we can't improve on our work, or change or grow. It just means that there is a certain signature way we are—the way we move or hold our head, the cadence of our speech, the way we dress, the way we laugh. I can see this right from the start in my classes. I have students do a drawing exercise on shape and value contrast on the first day. The instructions are simple with explicit rules and limits, and yet everyone does the exercise in a unique way. It is incredible to see. And I point that out to them, the beauty of that diversity of approach. Even if they can improve these drawings, there is some unique part of them that is different from the person sitting beside them and my goal is to take that uniqueness into account as we continue through the workshop. One way to tap into that uniqueness is to ask ourselves a series of questions, most importantly: 'What do we most love to paint?'.

When my children were younger and trying to decide what to study or what direction to follow, I would always tell them to follow their giggles. When we are on the right track, there is a gut feeling that is sort of bubbly, very much like giggling, and I advised them to follow that, which they have done. This is Joseph Campbell's expression, 'follow your bliss' integrated as a bodily sensation.

I tell my painting students about the importance of questioning themselves. I suggest they ask, 'What do I most want to paint right now?'. I go on to explain that it helps if they tell themselves that the choice doesn't have to be set in stone for the remainder of their lives. It's a choice for now. Follow that choice, I say. Make a body of work around it. For example, if they feel excited about working in black and white with strong value contrast, they should create a body of work with these limitations. I suggest that they make at least ten paintings, but it's best if they can make more, say twenty or thirty. As they go along, they'll see if the idea continues to excite them. If they get new ideas as they go for small variations on the theme, then they should really work the idea. I further suggest that after they've finished five or ten paintings, they should check in with themselves and if they're feeling bored or drained, it's a body signal for the time to consider a change.

I also encourage my students to allow themselves time to 'play' as artists, which will enable them to get out of their heads and in touch with their inner wisdom. While our personal voices are always there, it's sometimes hard to access them when our critical minds interfere. When we play, completing very small, quick, and free works, we release those inhibitions. When I am stuck sometimes, or between series, or even when searching for new ideas, I give myself unstructured time to play. I get out some Arches Oil Paper or Multimedia Artboard and make monotypes or small paintings, applying the paint in different ways, using colours I normally might not. I stretch myself and explore. I might never show this work to anyone, as I'm not thinking about a purpose or a product, or if I will get new ideas, or if I will show this work, or if I will sell it. I'm just playing—bringing passion and excitement into the work and feeling the vulnerability that comes with trying something new. Making art is combining that raw and playful quality with the techniques and experience we develop in pursuing the craft of painting.

Not every painting or work in progress needs to be exhibited in a show, or posted on social media. It's important not to show new work to people too soon. We need to develop the ideas first by ourselves. When I'm working on a new idea in my painting, I don't let anyone into my studio, not even my family. I don't want positive or negative comments. I don't want a smile or a frown or my interpretation of the responses. It's not wise to show work that is still raw and being developed. It's also wise not to post it on social media where we can count the likes and hearts, and think, 'it must be good if there are lots of likes, right?'. This will definitely influence the work, and we might never know where it could have gone had we let it grow wings.

When I go through a time of transition in my work and I'm not sure where my voice is or what I want to express, I find it helpful to turn to journal writing. It has always been an important way for me to understand myself. It helps me to see in another way and find answers I might not have expected. One thing I encourage my students to explore in their journals is the question, 'What is it that I love about painting?'. One woman wrote a wonderful children's story as she explored this query. The child in the story was shown to experience aspects of life—the touch of the wind and rain, and the sight of flowers in the fields in highly creative ways. The writing of the story reconnected this woman with the reason she loved making art in the first place. Small, wordless sketches can also be an important way to explore this question.

Looking at the work of important historical artists, as well as prominent contemporary painters and artists, is a vital part in learning about painting, not only to educate the eye, but also to learn who we are and what we like. I encourage my students to look at the art of others to assist in discovering their own style. I suggest that they write down what it is that they like about the work of those artists. I ask them to consider the qualities they like: Is it the meditative feeling, the use of bright hot colours, the sensitive use of line? I then invite them to think about whether they want those qualities in their own work, or do they enjoy that in the work of others but not necessarily in their own? When they come across the work of artists whose work they don't like, I ask them to think specifically about what it is about the work that they don't like. It's a way of learning about yourself as an artist through others. Choice. Choice. Choice. Who you are is defined by your choices.

Finding our own voice in art is just that. It's about the choices we make and then sticking with those choices long enough to explore them deeply.

Chapter 13:
A Question of Time

In the midst of winter, I finally found there
was within me an invincible summer.
—Albert Camus

A benefit of coming to art later in life is having the luxury of time to dedicate to developing our inner lives, the time to pick up that golden thread and follow it. But the scales of time give rise to an important question: Is there enough time left? While we finally have time to look into our souls, we may wonder if we have enough time to become proficient at an endeavour that takes time to learn.

On the positive side, that pressure serves as a vehicle for focus. That focus can be used to learn the craft while resisting the societal expectation of turning out a product. American respondent, Cynthia J. Lee addresses the topic in this way:

> Coming to art after age fifty, has given me a heightened appreciation for the importance of being fully present in the moment. Earlier decades held more daily responsibilities to others, and more distractions. With this leisurely stage of life, I have time to explore places, objects and events that capture my attention in the course of a

day. These explorations lead me into powerful themes and metaphors that I can then express in my art. This approach to life is immensely satisfying. I can savor the moment in ways that my younger, distracted self could not. With age and experience, I have come to know that I have an authentic personal voice, a story only I can tell. This is a humbling realization: I can express a point of view through my art that is unique to my understanding of the world around me.

Julie Brogan, a respondent from the US, also writes about the gift of time. "Time to work, travel for classes and afford art materials are a few of the benefits that I experience. I make art because I love it and I don't have to make a living at it."

There is also the push, pull of time. These are artists who are in that in-between space, where, at last, they have the freedom from employment and child-rearing and caring for parents, yet they know that their time is limited. Cynthia J. Lee says:

> There is a pressure that comes with advancing age. I am closer to the end of my life than the beginning. I often hear an inner mantra: 'Hurry up! Create more art! Faster!'. This impatience works against the quiet time necessary to hear my inner voice, and to delve into the deeper emotions which always feed the truest art.

I wrote to True Ryndes to check in with him as to where his life has taken him in the years since he had responded to my 2019 questionnaire. He wrote back to say that he and his partner moved into a retirement community and that he has a fabulous new studio, all wood and glass and air, that is reached by a dirt road. The move prompted him to go through his earlier work and to look back on the art of that slightly younger self. At that time, he had created a series of small, hard-edge paintings exploring the question as to whether that style of painting could hold the same emotional power as loosely brushed works. True goes on to say:

> In subsequent years I explored other roads into painting and acquired different tools, but most recently I have returned to the deceptive simplicity and language of the shadowed squares and a naturally-occurring variation: crossroads...Would this return have happened without our leaving friends and neighbors for a retirement community, without my having leukemia, without the gerbil wheel of social media, without the current degree of socio-political conflict, without the pandemic, without the gift of a new studio, without imagining the time limitations ahead? It's hard to say... but with this return has come a new sense of confidence about myself as an artist. Perhaps that's because I have a quantity of dedicated time to appreciate. I love connecting with that younger True and his vision. I have perspective on the links between my current works and those shadows under the table. Now, fourteen years later, I no longer feel like an imposter. Surprising to me... I also care far less about recognition and sales. I maintain a website, submit an occasional proposal, and exhibit when it's convenient, often with others.

As with life in general where balance is important, there are positives and negatives to becoming an artist later in life. We bring our life experience, our maturity, our ability to look at the big picture and recognize patterns. On the other hand, we can see the passage of time in our bodies, our energy, our health. We know we don't have fifty more years to develop our work. Geri De Gruy shares reflections about making art and both the pressures and joys of aging:

> Because I'm aging and death is closer and more real than it has ever been, I think I see more clearly, both with my

eyes and my heart...I'm willing to be still. I want to take it all in. I want to see the visible and the invisible.

James Edward Scherbarth, wrote in his response, "Time is a great motivator—when you realize that you are in the third act as they say, you become emboldened and clearer about what you want."

Many who responded to the questionnaire mentioned that health issues came along that compromised their dedication to their art practice. For some, the health issues and their lowered energy levels, prevented them from making much art. Others took their health issues as incentive. Respondent Susan Lindsay reflected:

> I had a life-changing health diagnosis fifteen years ago and I decided that I needed to embrace all those things that I had always wanted to do. While we all know we're going to die, we somehow deny it as though it's not going to happen to us. So while we can see the horizon getting closer as we age, it's not always a motivator. Or maybe it's procrastination that we fall back on—I can always work on that project next year.

Many of those who responded to my questionnaire mentioned that time was one of the challenges in coming to art later in life in that there wasn't enough time left.

According to Cousineau, "To have more time we have to make time, as counterintuitive as that may sound, by slowing down and stretching it. Or else you become a time-victim, a master procrastinator. You make sacred time by renewing yourself with solitude."[29] Let's not forget that while Vincent Van Gogh started painting at twenty-seven (much earlier in life than the subjects of my book), he only painted for a total of ten years! That's ten years from when he first picked up a paintbrush. Georges Seurat was a working artist for only nine years.

The question might be, can creativity occur without the deliberate use of time? Cousineau says, "Your image of time determines the intensity of your focus and the heat of your desire to be creative.

Commitment is the key."[30] I especially like these words of Mary Oliver, from her essay *Of Power and Time*: "The most regretful people on earth are those who felt the call to creative work, who felt their own creative power restive and uprising, and gave to it neither power nor time."[31]

Acutely aware of the passage of time, some older artists are more intense in their creative focus. None of us knows how much time we have left, so it's important to use each day.

Chapter 14 :
Fear

Why should we honour those that die upon the field
of battle? A man may show as reckless a courage in
entering into the abyss of himself.
—W. B. Yeats

Years ago, I had an artist residency in County Mayo, Ireland where I
stayed in a beautiful stone townhouse and painted in a separate studio.
On my first day there when I was unpacking my things and getting
settled in, I noticed something on a shelf in the kitchen. It was a small
heart-shaped stone made of slate that a previous artist must have
found and left there. On the stone the artist had scratched the words
'Be Brave.' I appreciated this gift from a stranger who knows that
making art takes courage.

Some of the respondents commented on courage. American artist
Suzanne Siegal states:

> It takes a lot of courage to create art. It's a long and
> tedious process that non-artists around me often don't
> understand. I have had to make it a priority even when it
> made little sense economically, and it was difficult to keep

going, knowing I have a lot less time as a result of starting late in life.

Lisa Boardwine, shares, "I have relentlessly pursued my life's dream and that takes courage and determination. It would have been easy to let the critics and non-supporters knock you down and cause you to stop pursuing an artistic journey."

The origin of the word courage is the French word *coeur*, or heart. In one of its earliest forms, the word courage meant to tell the story of who you are with your whole heart. More than a quality, courage is overcoming difficulty despite the presence of fear. Courage is having our first solo art show. It's changing directions in our work even if we have no idea where we are going or how we will get there, or if the work will be accepted; following our heart no matter where it leads and trusting that it knows the way; choosing a life in the arts even though it may not pay the bills. It takes determination to come to art late in life because no one else may support us on that journey.

Committing ourselves to the hard work required to become an artist creates change in our lives, and challenges the established patterns that others have come to expect from us. We set up routines for many aspects of our lives: how we structure our days, how we do our work, and how we relate to family and friends. We settle into a way of being that makes us feel safe and doesn't take up too much energy. As we grow older, routines become entrenched. So to become artists in later life—setting up studio space and spending hours each day working at our art—can throw a wrench not only into our daily habits but also into our relationships with others. Like throwing a pebble in a quiet pool, the ripples create new circles that affect others. Not only do we have to learn to see ourselves in another way—as artists—but so do the people around us. If our friends and loved ones fear our changing, they might want to hold us back. It's risky deciding to grow and change even in the face of resistance from others. It involves allowing them their feelings but choosing still to move forward to connect with our creative spirit.

Ted Butler, a Canadian respondent wrote:

> Many people around me didn't believe in me becoming an artist and some actually laughed. I also found that to be the case when I returned to school later in life. Maybe the laughter was their own insecurities coming out!

Annie Abdalla drew on her reserves of strength after friends questioned how she was spending her days when she switched from being a professor to doing art full time:

> The comment that I've heard from a few friends along the way that really gets under my skin [is], 'Oh so you're not working right now.' Jeesh, I'm working even harder than I did before! Maybe I give them the impression that I'm not working because my schedule is quite flexible now [before she entered Gampo Abbey]. I believe that the work I create is not just done in the studio, it's brewing all the time.

Gail Baar needed strength and determination to create her unconventional work when she was making quilts. She learned her craft in her thirties but didn't come to it as an art form until she was in her mid-fifties, after a career of teaching private cello lessons and playing in orchestras. In making her quilts, Gail focused on large, quiet, geometric shapes and strong contrast, unusual in a field where quilts are often highly patterned. She shares:

> My art is different from others. I had to be courageous just believing that this is the direction I wanted to go, to say this is art, this is who I am and what I want to say, even though it does not look like the art other quilters do.

Gail has also been fearless in transitioning from quilt making, where she had achieved success, into becoming a painter, continuing to grow, moving her art forward and allowing herself to be a beginner again.

Georgia O'Keeffe commented on courage:

> Being on the edge isn't always easy. In that place, where we're really striving and taking risks, we leave ourselves open to rejection. If we *are* rejected, the critical voice inside our heads may pipe up and add more disapproval. That's why it's good for artists to have some support on the path.[32]

This might involve finding like-minded artists through social media networking or joining local art groups. Our families too can sometimes be our biggest champions if we invite their support and keep them involved with our work, taking the time to explain to them what it's about and what we are aiming for.

Support and encouragement may come to us when we least expect it, providing us with the courage to carry on when things seem bleak. One day, several years ago, I received notice that my application to an artist residency I had sent in much earlier in the summer had been refused. I desperately hoped to go to this artist residency and expected to be accepted. Just before this, I was also rejected from a gallery I had applied to. I had just completed the work for my huge upcoming solo exhibition at a museum and should have been in a celebratory mood, but those two rejections threw me off and left me feeling utterly discouraged. I couldn't paint the rest of that day and the inner critic was loud in my ear. I got into my car that afternoon to do some errands and, as I turned on the engine, instead of music on the radio, I heard a deep male voice say, 'If you hear a voice in your head that says you cannot paint, then by all means paint, and that voice will be silenced.' Stunned by the synchronicity, I stopped the car to write that statement down. It was exactly what I needed to hear. When I came home, I looked up the quotation and found that it was by Van Gogh. Who better to offer these inspiring words that gave me the courage to carry on? Encouragement can come from anywhere if we're open to it.

"The only choice we have as we mature" writes poet David Whyte in his poem "Vulnerability", from his book *Consolations: The Solace, Nourishment and Underlying Meaning of Everyday Words:*

> is how we inhabit our vulnerability, how we become larger and more courageous and more compassionate through our intimacy with disappearance, with disappearance, our choice is to inhabit vulnerability as generous citizens of loss, robustly and fully, or conversely, as misers and complainers, reluctant and fearful, always at the gates of existence, but never bravely and completely attempting to enter, never wanting to risk ourselves, never walking fully through the door.[33]

It takes courage to see ourselves anew and to allow ourselves to be seen by others in a different way.

Chapter 15:
Regrets

My only regrets are my economies
(never my extravagances)—particularly those
of spirit and love.
—Doris McCarthy

With no formal training, Australian author Bronnie Ware found herself working in palliative care. During this time of looking after many dying people, Bronnie's life was transformed. As she lived and cared for the dying in their final months and days, Bronnie had deep and meaningful conversations with them. The patients shared with her their final thoughts about dying and their life regrets. In her book, *The Top Five Regrets of the Dying*, Bronnie reveals which regrets were most significant and suggests that the rest of us could try to address these issues in a positive way while we still have the time. The most common regret people articulated was not having had the courage to live their own lives, not the lives others expected of them.[34]

When I asked respondents to describe any regrets they might have at not making art until later in life, the responses were equally divided between no regrets and some regrets. Some responses were pragmatic. Mary Mirabel, an artist from the US, reflects:

I can't say I have any regrets as I wasn't 'called' to create art until late. I feel this gift was given to me at the time most appropriate for my life purpose. Earlier in my life I would have been too busy with my family and a career.

I feel exactly the same as Mary. I went to university, studied psychology, and had two children. They were still young when I started to paint, and I worked around their lives, between my job in psychology, driving them to their activities, helping with homework, and making meals, fitting in my art as I could. No regrets there, I just loved every minute I had to paint. And my children learned about painting with me as I painted on the kitchen counter or kitchen table between meal times. I remember my then twelve-year-old daughter passed behind me as I worked on a floral watercolour one evening and stopped to say, "Mum, I think you need more variety in the greens!" Then she smiled back at me cheekily as she walked away. Another respondent, US artist Susan Delgavis, says that she had no regrets. "I look at my transition from medicine to art as natural. In retrospect my life experiences were a preparation for becoming what I was always meant to be."

Many echoed this sentiment by indicating that art came into their lives when they were not only ready for it but also able to appreciate how much it enriched their lives. Annie Abdalla disavows any major regrets and acknowledges the main reason she had for not becoming an artist earlier in life:

> None at all. I really think I've benefited from the circuitous route that I've taken to get here. I have formal training in a smorgasbord of disciplines and these all serve to strengthen my ability to think and create... There are times when I listen to folks describe their experience of just wanting to draw when they were young—they knew from the very beginning that they wanted to be an artist. OK, maybe it does rattle me some days, perhaps a niggling concern that I don't have what it takes because it

didn't show up early. But honestly it just didn't occur to me that I could ever have these skills.

Other respondents had a few regrets. Some regretted that they had no art education; some that they wasted their time worrying about whether people liked their art; some that they felt they weren't good enough…or didn't have the talent…or had buried their creative side for so long. Canadian respondent Louise Lamirande writes:

> I have regrets for all the time denying my need to create and listening only to the destroying inner voice. I can only imagine where I would be professionally if I had not stopped painting all that time. However, I cannot deny the maturity gained through those years and life experiences.

American respondent Victoria Foster Harrison writes about a more particular regret: "My college degree ended at a Bachelors in General Art. I regret never pursuing a BFA or Masters, but I don't care to spend a minute dwelling on the situation." Like Victoria, many respondents indicated that they have only a few regrets, but they allow themselves only short forays into wondering, 'What if'? These 'what if' questions can crop up for us at certain stages: 'What if I'd taken a different path? What if I'd decided to study art therapy instead of taking the year off to work on my art? What if I'd gone to a different university or married someone else? How would my life be different?'.

Susan Cartwright, who in her previous lifetime was a senior federal public servant in the Canadian government, answered those questions in this way:

> Well, yes, in some ways [I have regrets]. But I also don't believe in regrets. I would not have met the man I have been married to for almost 40 years. I would not have had so many of the fantastic experiences I had through university and my work (I spent 21 years in the Foreign Service, including 15 years living overseas). I would not have been

made a member of the Order of Canada. I would not have met all the interesting people I have met. I might well have had other experiences and met other people, but it is hard comparing a known with an unknown. I am focussed instead on thinking how lucky I am (a) to still be alive 13 years after being diagnosed with IBC [Inflammatory Breast Cancer], (b) to have the opportunity and the means to pursue my art now, and (c) to revel in the pleasure it gives me.

Michela Sorrentino is more explicit about her regrets but ends up expressing a similar sentiment:

Sometimes I think about [regrets], (usually in the middle of the night when I have a bout of insomnia) and freak myself out thinking of all the years I had wasted not making art or regretting not having completed an art education BFA and MFA to give my art more clout with galleries and the art world. I sometimes count how many more art making years I have in me, hoping that I will be like Agnes Martin or Georgia O'Keeffe that were able to make art into their old age up to their last days...
I think about how everything happens for a reason and yes, maybe I did whittle away a few years in my youth but all those experiences have made me who I am today and today I am making art. That is what really counts.

Carol Retsch-Bogart, a US respondent, expresses that dichotomy regarding regrets commonly experienced by many of the respondents, and ends with an amusing image: "Yes and no... My regret would be if my aging body does not cooperate with my 'toddler' enthusiasm." Some respondents linger on the 'what ifs'. Others can't be bothered dwelling on regrets. Life has taken them in various directions that have enriched their lives and here they are now, combining their life experiences with learning about their creative selves and finding joy in the process.

Part IV
Coming to Art Later in Life: Supporting the Practice

Chapter 16:
Learning the Craft

Be a good craftsman;
it won't stop you from being a genius.
—Pierre-Auguste Renoir

There are four practices that I feel are most important to the development of an artist and what I aim to teach in my workshops. They are: learning the craft; listening to inner guidance; allowing creative play; and committing to the work through discipline.

While art can be fun and engage an artists' whole soul, it isn't easy; it isn't only exciting or therapeutic. The place to start is to acquire technique. We have to set up a studio, do the work, and put in the hours. It takes a long time to learn a trade or to acquire the skills of a carpenter or a surgeon; art is no different. If we learn the skills first, then we will be free to explore. "To do anything artistically you have to acquire technique, but you create *through* your technique, not *with* it,"[35] wrote musician Stephen Nachmanovitch in his book, *Free Play: Improvisation in Life and Art*.

In his book, *Dancing with the Gods, Reflections on Life and Art*, Kent Nerburn cautions artists not to be in too much of a hurry. "As young [or emerging] artists, we are too quick to want to run to the well of pure creative expression. We do not want to subject ourselves to training that seems to run contrary to the creative fire that burns inside us."[36]

I was in that kind of hurry when I began painting as an older artist. I felt that I'd better just get going and start expressing myself, seeing I'd come to painting so late in life. At first I just jumped in to painting in watercolours without doing any of the careful drawing my instructors did, thinking that I'd be much more expressive. I was making watery blobs of washed-out colour over the whole surface of the paper. While that was fun, I gradually came to realize that I needed to learn how to draw (at least for the sort of painting I wanted to do at the time). I signed up for an evening life-drawing class at a college not far from home. The slow sustained poses of the voluptuous model were a delight to draw as well as the quick gestural poses of the tall, muscular man. Over a long period of time, my drawing improved. Then I came to realize that I needed to learn about colour and took a week-long class in mixing colour and learning the various aspects of colour.

A would-be artist may have the most profound visions, feelings, and insights but without skill, there is no art. The requisite variety that opens up our expressive possibilities comes from practise, play, exercise, exploration, and experimentation. Jazz pianist Kenny Werner writes in his book, *Effortless Mastery: Liberating the Musician Within:*

> There is a long-standing controversy about technique versus creativity. One camp says, I don't want to absorb too much technique, too much language because it will squelch my creativity. Some people are afraid to learn too much for fear of losing their soul. But that doesn't hold up. What could the poet or playwright write without command of the language? Composer Donald Erb says that 'if your talent can't stand a little training it must be pretty fragile to begin with'. The other camp states, 'I play bebop well, therefore I am an artist.' But that doesn't hold up either. Can you say, 'I speak English well therefore I am

an artist? Of course not. It all depends on what you say with language. Being able to speak in sentences is a skill. Being a painter, a poet, a sculptor—that is art.[37]

Part of learning the craft is learning to make choices, learning how to set limits to work within them. Life is made up of choices. Endless choices, from the daily, to the long-term. By our senior years we've had plenty of experience in making choices. Getting into art, though, opens up a whole new world of choices. Besides the core issue of deciding what your message is in your painting, there are endless other choices to be made. For example, which art materials to use: oil, cold wax medium and oil, encaustic, acrylic, watercolour, pastel, ink, among many others. As well, there are choices within each of these materials: heavy body acrylics, soft body acrylics, high flow, slow drying, and on and on. Then there's the question of how one should apply them? Some people try all the mediums, buying the gamut of art supplies. There's an endless variety of paper, canvas, wood panels, multimedia artboard, as well as tools for applying the paint. Then there is the choice of which instructor, each with their own particular skill and focus. Some people trail endlessly from one art workshop to another, dragging along the full bag of art supplies required for that class. This is the paradox of choice—having so many options should give freedom, but it can confuse. Creativity begins with making choices. It comes from establishing limits, not endless freedom.

Stephen Nachmanovitch states :

> Sometimes we damn limits, but without them art is not possible. They provide us with something to work with and against. In practising our craft we surrender, to a great extent, to letting the materials dictate the design. Limits yield intensity. Working within the limits of the medium forces us to change our own limits. Improvisation is not breaking with forms and limitations just to be 'free' but using them as the very means of transcending ourselves.[38]

Limitations might seem restrictive but instead they help us by putting constraints on our choices, offering us the freedom to explore more deeply. Working within those limits, the artist can find a way of working that they love, one that is stimulating and exciting. Once they have found it, they should commit themselves to it and develop a long series of paintings using the ideas they've been working on.

The numerous advantages of working in a series are detailed by art consultant and author Alan Bamburger in his essay, *Reasons to Make Art in a Series*. He explains:

> The problem with the 'make whatever I feel like making whenever I feel like making it' approach to art is that when everything is different and there's no common thread, it's difficult for us to get a grip on where you're going, what you stand for, what your art is about. Viewers try their best to sift through everything and make sense of it, but if no clear order, pattern or intent is evident, they basically give up. When each consecutive piece is different from all those that precede it, viewers have to start fresh with every new image, resulting in a start, stop, start, stop, start, stop process of trying to understand every one from scratch, and then trying to figure out how they all fit together with the rest. That's not only time consuming and labor intensive, but it's also difficult, confusing and in many cases, ultimately exhausting.
>
> When I ask artists why they create art this way, they often say they want to make sure they have something for everyone. This strategy may make sense them but unfortunately, way more often than not, they end up with nothing for anyone. People are either overwhelmed by the variety, or they don't have the have time and energy to look at and analyze every single piece, or they can't get a handle on what the artists' overall identities or purposes

are, or they're so inundated with options that they can't make up their minds what they like most or why they like it. Way too many choices...[39]

The process is about being able to explore, investigate, examine or address particular ideas, themes, issues, compositions, concepts or topics in progressively deeper and more meaningful ways, and from a greater variety of perspectives than is possible by making just one or two.

It's a difficult point to make to students that they work in a series, because I think they expect that their unique way of working will suddenly come to them as though anointed with a fairy wand. And once anointed, they won't have to do the search to find out what they want to say and how to say it. I see students jump from one idea, one medium (watercolour, oils, acrylics), one way of working, to another. In doing that, they must become beginners again in this new way of working.

The Icelandic artist Georg Gudni, who died at age fifty in 2011, made a difficult choice about his subject matter. In his book, *Strange Familiar: The Work of Georg Gudni,* he wrote about how he decided to turn away from what he was seeing in contemporary art. Even though he worried that it would be difficult to say anything new about landscape, he decided to try anyway. And as he did, he realized how deeply connected he was to the land and, therefore, to the work. By checking in with his heart, and trusting what he felt, he went on to create beautiful, ethereal landscapes of his native Iceland. He described his process: "I paint the mountain with myself / I paint myself into the mountain / I paint the mountain from myself."[40]

Trust in ourselves, in our feelings is sometimes so difficult to do. When I'm in a fallow period with my work, I have to trust that the energy, the ideas will return. That's not an easy time. At those times, even if I show up regularly in my studio, the work just doesn't have any energy behind it. The ideas are gone. The muse has flown. All I can do is keep working and wait patiently.

Patience is another important part of learning the craft. Interestingly, it also seems to be a lesson that we get from art as older artists. This surprised me. Perhaps patience is on the list of life lessons because when we older artists finally come to art, when life has released us from the need to make money, to care for younger and older family members, and has birthed us into a new life, we just want to get at it. We get up, dust off all our earlier worries and cares, and find inside a freedom to begin to paint. We're ready now. Let's not waste time.

Michela Sorrentino shares:

> [I've learned] to be more patient. Not to give up. To give it time. If something is not working in a painting, move on to another and come back to that painting the next day. The painting will show me the way. These are all lessons I can take into my everyday life. I'm more forgiving and patient with the people in my life.

I'm not the most patient person. My kids will attest to that. I've been forced to learn some patience in order to become a painter. Endless patience is required, and stubborn perseverance. Many years ago I broke my wrist on my painting arm. Laid up with a swollen foot as well as the broken wrist, I was unable to paint. I decided to be patient and work on the tedious task of bringing my inventory up to date. Then, as I finished that task, I took down some books on composition from my bookshelf to spend time refreshing myself on the basic skills of painting. What I learned helped me deepen my teaching and gave me ideas I could pass on to my students. My being confined to a chair, a task that was routine and boring, fostered new skills I could use in my teaching.

A similar thing happened when we were locked down with COVID-19. I could feel the anxiety in the air, the fear, the uncertainty. While some artists found the solitude and quiet time a great opportunity to work in their studios, I felt stifled by the fear and anxiety in the world around us. I became creative in another way, though, as I developed and taught Zoom workshops where artists gave feedback to one another. I moved my Workshops in Wild Places travel project onto Zoom as well, and taught ways of connecting in a much deeper way to nature and translating that into abstract paintings. During the preparation required for the classes, my own connection with nature deepened though meditative walking in the woods behind my home and through reading and developing exercises to support participants in enriching their own connection with nature. I trusted that something positive would come out of the adversity of the pandemic.

That idea of trust, reminds me of a battle I had with a robin a few years ago. She was trying to build her nest on the ledge of the transom above my front door. Each day she brought endless amounts of debris from my garden and each day, I used my broom to sweep it away. She, or maybe it was another robin, had built her nest in the exact place two years before and for a few weeks I couldn't use the front door. But the worst of it was that in that precarious place, one of the babies had fallen to its death. I didn't want to have that happen again, so I kept sweeping away the grasses and each day she brought more. We were both determined. Then one weekend I was away for three days, and when I came home, Boom! There was a solid, mud-packed nest. I climbed a ladder inside my house and peered into the nest through the transom window. Five small blue eggs nestled in the bottom.

I was fearful for the robin's creative work because the ledge on which the nest was built was only six-inches deep. The robin approached her creativity with full trust and optimism and dogged determination. Within a short time, four of the eggs hatched, grew wings and flew away. The fifth did not hatch. It remained in the nest as a turquoise reminder of unborn dreams. And now, as I look at my artwork, I wonder in what way I might be limiting myself or not trusting.

Matthew Fox, a theologian writes in his book, *Creativity: Where the Divine and Human Meet,* about how a lack of trust keeps us wallowing in our non-creative state. He refers to the book, *The Poetics of Space,* by Gaston Bachelard, who writes about trust:

> Trust can begin with the simple act of examining a bird's nest, for when we examine a nest, we place ourselves at the origin of confidence in the world... Would a bird build its nest if it did not have its instinct for confidence in the world? A nest is a sign of optimism. It knows nothing of the hostility of the world... A dreamer might say that the world is the nest of mankind. For the world is a nest and an immense power holds the inhabitants of the world in this nest. And with this trust, creativity and imagination come to life.[41]

If we are to follow the gold thread, follow our creative passion, our first task is to learn the craft, put in the time, learn the necessary skills. As we begin to paint, we realize other skills are necessary too—we need to learn to focus, to make choices, and to set artistic limits for ourselves. As older artists, we need to trust ourselves, believe in our own wise council, and have patience and confidence that life is unfolding as it should.

Chapter 17:
Listening to Your Inner Guidance

I think a good way to conceive of sacred space
is as a playground. If what you're doing seems like play,
you are in it.
—Joseph Campbell

A second supporting practice and an important one is learning to listen to our inner guidance. There are some methods available to us and some practices or rituals that other artists do that can be helpful to take us to a deeper place within, a place where we get out of the way and let the inner artist take over. Artists often aim for that place of inspiration where art enters us and we become the vessel for its creation. This is the state in which we lose track of time, following where the work leads. Then, oh yes, *then*, is the moment we've been waiting for, when it feels like the planets are in alignment. That's the place where the work takes flight. It's ours no longer.

Early Greeks and Romans believed in the idea of a genius. Not the sort of genius we speak of today referring to someone who is incredibly brilliant, but the idea that people are born with the protection of a specific genius, their own private divine entity who attends and watches over them. Their ideas came from their genius and the credit or dispar-agement of their work would also be attributed to their genius.[42]

Another term for this is the muse—a term that anthropologist, Angeles Arrien, traces back to the Greek meaning one who can 'inspire our soul and ignite our creativity.' The muses were portrayed as nine women, the daughters of Memory, who lead us down the road of creativity. The muses were said to provide unceasing inspiration to any soul who sincerely evokes their integrity and creativity.[43]

In Greek and Roman times, one would enter a creative space inspired by one's personal genius or your muse. Psychologists call this space flow[44] ; musicians talk about it as the zone. This is the place where you feel taken up and used for what feels like a higher purpose, as though being held in the hand of something greater than yourself, where that inner critic is moved aside and you become a channel for creativity.

Philip Guston, Canadian American painter and printmaker, report-edly said that when he walked into his studio late at night to paint, it was always full of people—friends and associates, dealers, critics, the ghosts of living and dead artists. As he started work, one by one they would get bored and slip away, until he was left alone with his brushes and his canvas. If he was lucky, he would disappear too.[45]

Scientists attempt to study this otherworldly experience. An experiment at John Hopkins hospital involved six pianists playing a keyboard while undergoing fMRI scanning. When they improvised on their own—the keystone of all kinds of creativity—the musicians' brains went into a "dissociated frontal activity state"—like being in the zone. Neurological activity associated with self-monitoring and inhibition decreased. The pianists' brains didn't respond the same way when they played a standard tune[46] It's the same energy that musi-cians talk about when they do an entire recording in a few hours. Flow has happened.

From time to time, I experience flow when I'm painting in my studio. It comes as a gift. It comes when we're creating art (or meditating, walking, or swimming, whatever keeps us in the moment). It arrives unexpectedly, a gentle grace. We can't make it stay and we're aware of its presence only when it's gone, when we're left with a sense that we were touched by the divine.

I've had this happen a few times in my painting career. A painting came very easily and beautifully, at a skill level way beyond where I was at the time. It took my breath away. I would then try to reach that level again. It took a lot of work to create other paintings that were at that level of skill. After a year or so, I created at that level more consistently. And then, grace visited again with other paintings that were, again, beyond my skill level at the time, showing me where I needed to go. After those experiences, I wondered if it was possible, if not to make the experience happen again, at least to open the door to embrace this kind of gift.

I realized that while I can't summon the flow state, I can create conditions that allow it—I can invite the genius, the muse—I can invite flow into my studio and my process. This invitation consists of my intention coupled with some practices that I do to prepare for work. You might call them rituals.

I have a worn-out comfortable chair near the door of my studio. The chair itself feels like a sacred space. My ritual when I go into the studio to paint each day is to sit in that chair and light a candle and place it on the small table beside the chair. Centring myself in meditation, I sit back, close my eyes, take some deep breaths, and gently bring my attention into my studio, into my body. Some days I imagine a ball of light on top of my head that I inhale into my body, watching it slowly move down my body with each breath, calming me and filling me with light. Often, I read a poem or write in my journal. When I feel centred and present to the studio space, I'm ready to begin.

Creating a ritual of preparation is an important part of the process to welcome creation, to put us inside the act of creation where we are not the maker, but art is revealed through us. Rituals, or specific routines that we perform before we begin our day in the studio, help us to enter that state of deep communion with self, the state of flow or, or as some call it, grace.

I talked about artist rituals in a workshop I taught, and I asked the artists in the class to write about their rituals. For Canadian artist Wendy Robertson, studio time begins first of all with organizing and getting her materials ready. Then, she explains, "I light a candle on my desk where I sit to do my meditation." She gets comfortable in her desk chair and turns on her Tibetan bells meditation music. She says:

> I deep breathe several times, visit each chakra, finishing with the crown [chakra], surrendering to the higher energies where I just 'hang out' until I feel I am ready to paint. Before starting [to paint], I make notes if I receive images or information during my meditation… I almost always listen to ambient music while I work, which helps me stay in a meditative zone.

Canadian artist, Leona Brown explains her ritual:

> I get down to the studio at 1 p.m. as I am a nighthawk not a morning person. The first thing I do as I cross the threshold of the studio door, I say out loud 'I'm home.' I really feel as if this sacred space is home, where I can be me…truly me. It's a spontaneous outcry that is felt very deeply. Next, I turn on the heater, put on my apron and assess the pile left over from the previous day. While gazing at the work I rearrange the jars and pots of paints, putting the labels all facing me. I line up the brushes, and scrappers, and knives, while sipping on chilled coffee.

Canadian respondent, Cathy Francis, writes that she begins her day by first sitting at her desk with her coffee:

> …Looking out on quite a beautiful view, looking at an image of curled fall grass, and a dry beech leaf, imagining the sound of rustling dried beech leaves in the winter. But

along with my new ritual there is what comes before: a bit of art education. This morning it was a short video.

Then she goes for a morning walk to the lake or through the woods before beginning. She explains that the most important part of the ritual for her is "opening the doors [to my studio] where I enter an atmosphere created by the things that I love, from books, to binders, along with inspirations and influences from ceramics, to props from the bookshop [Cathy used to own]. An odd studio, but mine."

Some artists have very elaborate rituals to begin the days in their studios, all with the purpose of centering themselves and hoping, I believe, to encourage the mystery of art to pay a visit. Suzanne Dvorak, an American artist comments, "My painting studio is on the lower level of our house. So my transition ritual begins before I go downstairs. After I meditate and before going downstairs I make some strong, black, sludge-like coffee." Once in the studio, Suzanne putters, arranging her paints and greeting her painting by rubbing it, engaging with the surface. She says, "I usually ask the painting a question or two: consider where it wants to go, and how we're going to move forward together." By this time the dog has settled on to his mat and Suzanne is ready to sit down at her desk for a brief time, sipping her coffee while she settles in, writing, drawing, or reading. She says:

> I'm transitioning, settling in. When I'm ready to actively paint I turn on the radio, usually listening to NPR—I'm used to the voices, the routine of the radio schedule, and I find that it is just enough of a distraction that I don't think too much about what I'm painting. The final step, which marks the biggest and final transition, is to put on one of my two studio aprons. I find it hard to paint if I don't have an apron on. If I do nothing else, I put on an apron. Then I begin to paint.

Accessing that flow place, where we disappear into the work, into the mystery of it, is not something that can be prescribed. It can't be forced. It can only be allowed, and that requires that we create an open space in our hearts and very intentionally invite it.

Meditation is a perfect way to learn to open up, to surrender and perhaps to invite that flow to enter. Mindfulness and meditation are entwined but different. Meditation is a practice where a person sits in a quiet place and takes time to turn inward, using a technique such as focusing on a mantra or listening to a guided meditation in order to achieve a state of focus, calmness, and clarity. Mindfulness is a quality of paying attention in daily life, gently pulling our attention back from wandering thoughts into the present moment, in whatever activity we might be doing, whether talking to a loved one or making dinner.

I've meditated for most of my life. I find, among other positives, it enhances my focus when I paint, and makes me more resilient to having bad days in the studio. I was introduced to Transcendental Meditation in the late sixties when Maharishi Mahesh Yogi brought it to North America. I practised TM for many years. Then in the mid-nineties, I was introduced to shamanic journeying at a workshop in Ireland, which, among other inner work, included an intro to shamanism. Being a visual person, I was well-suited to shamanism. I could easily visualize. Sandra Ingerman, a highly regarded long-time instructor of shamanism and author of many books on the topic, describes shamanic journeying as "techniques used by shamans worldwide to connect with spiritual helpers, to access personal spiritual guidance and healing, to help others and the planet and to reconnect with nature, its cycles and rhythms."[47] I studied shamanism with Sandra Ingerman and the Foundation for Shamanic Studies and practised it for many years. During COVID-19, I found the need to meditate in a group and joined an online interfaith meditation community, Meditation Chapel, which does a form of meditation called Centring Prayer.

While it's idyllic to think we stay in a calm, mindful place as we paint, there are times when our work isn't going so well and out of frustration we start making quick and angry marks. When that happens, our bodies get tight and our marks echo that tightness. It's a good idea to stop then and recentre ourselves to bring our attention back to the present. A good time to go outside for a walk. When things are going well, we're in the flow of ideas, living in the swirling, exciting energy of creativity.

Mindfulness also involves acceptance, meaning that we pay attention to our thoughts and feelings without judging them—without believing, for instance, that there's a 'right' or 'wrong' way to think or feel in a given moment. When we practise mindfulness, our thoughts tune into what we're sensing in the present moment rather than rehashing the past or imagining the future. Though it has its roots in Buddhist meditation, a secular practice of mindfulness has entered the American mainstream in recent years, in part through the work of Jon Kabat-Zinn and his Mindfulness-Based Stress Reduction (MBSR) program, which he launched at the University of Massachusetts Medical School in 1979. Since that time, thousands of studies have documented the physical and mental health benefits of mindfulness in general and MBSR in particular, inspiring countless programs to adapt the MBSR model for schools, prisons, hospitals, veterans centres, and beyond. On his website, mindful.org, Kabat-Zinn describes mindfulness as the "awareness that arises through paying attention, on purpose, in the present moment, non-judgementally."[48]

A myriad of health benefits are attributed to the practice of meditation and mindfulness, including a powerful effect on creativity. Being in the present moment is not only the practice of mindfulness, a goal in Buddhism, but also the practice of gratitude and the practice of creating art. Art is also a spiritual practice. Central to an art practice is staying in the moment. It's easy when we begin to paint because we can become so enthralled with the process and the materials—the way the watercolors blend together, or the way we can scrape back the oil and cold wax mixtures to reveal under layers, or the way we can apply stencils to molding paste to make textures that we can paint over, or the way that wax melts when heated. All of this is so engaging that we are automatically in the moment. Later though, when we've become used to the materials, when we're trying to create a painting, we realize we need to learn more skills and learn how to incorporate those skills in our work. This is the hard but necessary part. As we focus on learning those skills, our ability to be in the present can wane, the fun can start to go out of the work. It then becomes a chore as we try to remember the skills and still create an expressive painting. Best then to return to play, where we lose ourselves in the work again. Now though, we lose ourselves in a mindful way, combining the skills with play. Holding the balance.

Thanks to the consciousness-raising movement of the sixties and seventies, there are multiple ways of doing inner work, including yoga, shamanism, Tibetan Buddhism, Transcendental Meditation, contemplative Christianity, and Qi Gong. All of them involve staying in the moment, letting go of thoughts. Meditation helps not only with staying calm in the face of stress and frustration, improving our attention span, but also with incorporating divergent thinking. It opens our minds to new ideas. For example, in my meditation practice, while I focus on letting my thoughts go, sometimes there is what I call a bigger thought that just sits there, waiting for me, as though it can only be reached when I let go of small thoughts. Sometimes it comes as a vision of a painting, sometimes as an idea to pursue in a book or a blog post. I look at the vision as though it's a possible idea to explore. The American abstract painter Agnes Martin, often referred to as a minimalist, regularly had extremely detailed visions of paintings she thought she was to create. She would measure off the canvas into carefully delineated grids following what she saw in her visions.[49]

Meditation and art have long been associated and while art itself is considered by many to be a meditative experience, there are many artists who pursue meditation outside of their art practice. Some well-known artists who practise or practised meditation are Leonard Cohen, David Lynch, Yoko Ono, and Jack Kerouac.

The first time I taught a workshop outside my studio it was in a nearby art centre. I decided to begin each day with a guided meditation. I remember being particularly nervous about the meditation, more so than about the material I was going to teach. I worried that the students would find me too 'out there', doing meditation in an art class. But I was also proud of myself for having the courage to do that. I didn't receive any negative responses from them, just acceptance. After the meditation, I went on to teach the workshop. A couple of days later, I heard from the organizer that the group enjoyed the workshop, and what they liked best were the meditations! (I wasn't quite sure what that said about my teaching.) Now, many years later, I still open each day in my workshops with a meditation. I can feel the group energy change as they bring their focus into the studio or into the Zoom room.

A famous quote by Vietnamese Buddhist monk, peace activist and author Thich Nhat Hahn, was recently included in an article in the *New York Times* as a tribute to his life:

> To meditate means to go home to yourself. Then you know how to take care of the things that are happening inside you, and you know how to take care of the things that happen around you… Just be. Just being in the moment in this place is the deepest practice of meditation.[50]

I've found meditation to be helpful in my life in many ways, calming me when I've gone through periods of grief, anxiety, and fear, allowing creative ideas to percolate and, often, getting in touch with the deep core of me, when my mind settles and thoughts pass through. It's helpful for artists to learn to listen to our inner guidance to help us become a vessel for creativity, letting go of inhibition and the inner critical voice. Meditation and mindfulness can help prepare us, and while we can't *make* flow happen, we can create rituals to invite it in.

Chapter 18:
The Importance of Play

We don't stop playing because we grow older,
we grow older because we stop playing.
—George Bernard Shaw

A third way of supporting our art practice is through purposeful play, that emphasizes imagination and exploring boundaries, letting go of perfectionism. When musicians work, no matter the style, it's called playing. For others, play is often looked upon as a children's activity, not to be taken seriously. Play is different from game. In playing, we feel free, unhindered, uninhibited, as we explore joyfully. A game is a competition, with participants, following a set of rules, as in basketball or tennis. It may or may not be joyful. Ideas for paintings may or may not come from play, but the doing of it releases our conscious minds and lets ideas play with each other. It's difficult to teach people to play. Many of us have forgotten how. It's been trained out of us. As children, we were taught to colour within the lines, not to explore or make a mess. Unless we were taught to improvise while playing music, or to experiment while in art school, it's likely that the freedom of play, the source of our creative flame, was simply blown out. We became, instead, people of facts and information. But as Stephen Nachmanovitch explains, "Full-blown artistic creativity takes place when a trained and skilled grown-up is able to tap the source of clear, unbroken play-consciousness of the small child within."[51]

In my art classes, when I suggest beginning each studio day with play, many of the older people I teach don't know where to begin. They ask me to *show* them how to play. They've sadly forgotten or they've built a high wall to protect that vulnerable childlike part of themselves. I try to demonstrate how I play. But of course that's not exactly how I play when I'm by myself with no one leaning over my shoulder taking notes.

Play is about process, not product. It is the basis of creativity, the seed factory in which ideas germinate. When I play, I do it in private, not in front of a class, because it calls for me to go deep inside myself, to reconnect with that inner child who can be exuberantly and vulnerably silly. I close the door of my studio. I have no expectations for this work. No judgment, no goal. I bring out all my tools, all my paints, inks, mediums, paint sticks, pencils, then reach for something and begin. I always paint on small sheets of paper when I play so that the materials don't inhibit me with their preciousness. Playing initially on a large canvas or piece of paper is inhibiting because of its size and expense. I don't want to mess up such a large surface. So I work small, maybe on a 6 x 6 surface. I have lots of paper cut up and piled on the worktable beside me. Or I take sheets from a sketchbook and divide the paper in four with masking tape. Sometimes I allow myself only a short amount of time, say one minute (or less) to do all four sections so my head won't get involved and take over adding in tiny, picky marks.

Deb Clegg, a Canadian artist sent me a list of suggestions for play exercises to use to start a day in the studio:

- Rotate the paper often, change direction and tools—set timer for 1 minute between changes

- Choose three colours

- Draw and paint to music

- Scribble

- Close your eyes and make marks and lines

- Use your non-dominant hand

- Stand at a distance away from paper and use long-handled brush

- Use a palette knife

- Scratch into thick paint

There is no judgment involved in play and I expect nothing of it. Maybe the play will teach me something I can bring into my other work or maybe not. Think of the way children play. They put their whole focus into it. It's serious business. And then they're done. Gone. Off to something else, expecting nothing of the play activity, holding onto nothing. We're not children, but we can be just as intensely focused and wildly experimental in our play. I think of the architect Frank Gehry in the video *Sketches of Frank Gehry*. As he works on ideas for his buildings, he plays with bending strips of paper into shapes. This sort of play gave him the idea to create the bending steel structure of Guggenheim Museum Bilbao in Spain and the chairs made of bent, curved strips of wood, and the wiggle chairs as he calls them, made of many layers of laminated cardboard. He calls what he does 'serious play', which is what children do too, don't they? [52]

Marilyn Joyce is a US artist who knows how to play. In her response to my questionnaire she indicated that she makes constructions with paper she has dyed. She collects natural plant materials from her country property—leaves, roots, bark, and needles from various evergreen trees, as well as found earth pigments—and makes watercolours and dyes. She does test after test, looking for the colour of the dye as well as the strength of the colour and the permanence of it. Generally the dyes turn out to be soft colours with the feel of watercolours. Once she has dyed the papers the colours she likes, she then plays with the arrangement of the various sizes and shapes of the paper, perhaps adding thread or other natural fibers to create constructions as delicate as the wing of a butterfly.

A major component of play is surrender. Surrender is difficult to explain and often difficult to accomplish. We know when we've achieved it because we can feel it. It's a feeling of relaxing into the acceptance of what is. It's not a giving up or a reluctant giving in. There will come a time in play and in the painting process when we want to switch to making it be what we want it to be instead of letting the free painting lead the way. When we are in control mode, it feels like paddling upstream, fighting the current. The canoe is going nowhere. If you pull your paddle out of the water, let the canoe turn around and go with the current instead, you're in the energy of surrender. It's a whole different feeling.

I recognize two kinds of play. Perhaps there are more. There is the childlike play where the artist adds lines, textures, shape, or colours in a completely random, unconscious way, simply focusing on the process. Then there is mindful play which combines the non-thinking part of our brains with the skills of the craft. Perhaps that's what architect Frank Gehry means by 'serious play'. It involves preparing ourselves in an inner way, calming our minds and bringing ourselves into the present moment. It also involves coming to the work after having integrated the rules of composition. It's not *thinking* about those rules: we have incorporated that knowledge and then we let it go. In the same way, we can't pick up a saxophone and become jazz musicians by blowing random notes. Jazz has structure and skill behind it and the musician moves beyond that in order to fly.

My process of play involves opening myself and staying in that place for a while, letting energy move through me like a conduit as I paint. I don't seem to be able to stay in that space a long time. I try to be aware when it's present and when it leaves, and I try not to hold it longer than it wants to be there. I call it mindful play. Mindful painting.

Truly creative results happen by grace rather than effort and planning. Being present during the process of creation is one of the most essential skills of the artist. That, and letting go of our desires for a particular outcome, a product. Letting go also of our need for perfection.

Imperfection is what has made the world, claims the late astrophysicist Stephen Hawking in his YouTube video *An Imperfect Universe:*

> One of the basic rules of the universe is that nothing is perfect. Perfectionism simply doesn't exist. It was the way that gravity acted on the uneven surfaces of the gases that made up our universe, that created the Earth, the Moon, the planets, and the galaxies. Gravity cannot function without imperfection. So, the next time someone tells you that you've made a mistake, tell them that may be a good thing because without imperfection, neither you nor I would exist.[53]

It's so freeing to know this. And in the world of creativity, it's very freeing to actually try to make mistakes. In a photography book I have, one of the exercises is to shoot the worst photos you can. It brings a whole new outlook and playfulness. You lose sight of 'the product' or trying to take the perfect image.

One time when I was in an outdoor summer school painting class for adults, a few of us sat beside each other painting images of the shop across the road in a market area. The student beside me had a large sheet of Arches Watercolour paper attached to the board on his lap. He sat there in frustrated indecision, unable to begin, afraid to make a mistake on this perfectly clean paper. The instructor came by on his bike to check on how each of us was doing and to offer instruction. The student grew increasingly anxious, but couldn't begin. Finally, on the third time around on his bike route, the instructor, in complete frustration with the student, threw the remains of his cup of coffee on the white page. We all gasped in horror, looking at the student to see his reaction. He was livid. Furious! But it woke him up to see what he was doing. The teacher didn't apologize; he just rode off. After a while of huffing indignantly, the student eventually recovered. He used the energy of his anger and turned it around to create the best painting he'd done in that class. The teacher destroyed the 'perfection' that the student was battling.

In his book, *Coaching the Artist Within: Advice for Writers, Actors, Visual Artists and Musicians from America's Foremost Creativity Coach,* Eric Maisel offers a beneficial insight:

> To create we have to take the bad with the good. If we try to write only the good paragraphs, we are three-quarters of the way toward paralysis. The name that we've coined for this problem is 'perfectionism.' But it isn't that people afflicted this way are striving to be perfect. They are just striving to be good, which would be no problem at all, if only they also had internal permission to be bad.[54]

From my experience in teaching artists, I've witnessed the benefit that comes to artists if they adopt an attitude of acceptance and give themselves license to be 'bad' as defined by Maisel. I often hear artists verbally beating themselves up, sometimes speaking aloud so that the rest of us can hear, saying things like, 'What a mess I make,' 'I really hate this,' or 'What am I doing?' They're basically saying, 'I'm not good enough.' One of my recent students berated herself continually for three and a half days of my four-day workshop. She was extremely frustrated that her work wasn't going as she had planned, even though she was new to the cold wax and oil process I was teaching. I urged her to be more gentle with herself, but she seemed unable to stop. Finally, on the morning of the fourth day when she was totally frustrated and ready to listen, I suggested that she work very quickly without thinking, giving herself permission to make 'bad work. I also recommended that she open up to gratitude by silently thanking the work and the process for teaching her about painting. Finally, exhausted from the tension she'd created in fighting herself and the work, she simply surrendered to the process. In the last half day of the class, the tension released and she worked like a tornado. I could almost see the papers and tools swirling in the air around her. And just in the very last moments of the class, as the dust settled, we saw that with her new attitude of acceptance, she had produced some really exciting work.

In Japan, *Kintsugi* is the art of repairing broken bowls with gold. It draws attention to the fact that the bowl was broken and is then mended, making the bowl much more beautiful. The process shows acceptance of the imperfect, a way of saying that your scars are beautiful. The idea also relates to authenticity, acceptance that we'll never be able to paint the perfect image that we can see in our minds, but our attempt is what is important. It's similar to acceptance of the aging process in ourselves, our wrinkles, our grey hair, our fallen arches, our failing eyesight but, along with that, the depth of the inner lives that we've developed. It means caring for ourselves but accepting the changes. As Leonard Cohen puts it in his song *Anthem,* "There's a crack in everything, that's how the light gets in."

Miles Davis comments, "Do not fear mistakes. There are none." If you're an improvising musician or performer, setbacks or challenges can be the stuff of creativity. Mostly it brings you into the present moment. It calls for instantaneous creativity and the brain loves a challenge. It's exciting.

Letting go of rules and boundaries and the restrictions of perfectionism, and letting ourselves play can keep us in the moment, liberating our imaginations to explore new creative ideas.

Chapter 19:
Discipline/Commitment

Discipline is not the enemy of enthusiasm.
—Joe Clark

Every kind of music has its own soul Quincy.
It doesn't matter what style it is, just be true to it.
—Ray Charles (age 16) giving advice to Quincy Jones
(age 14)

The fourth practice for artists is to make a decision to commit to their art. No one improves without the discipline of putting in the time to improve their skill. These respondents discussed the importance of discipline and commitment.

- "I have learned how to prioritize my studio time, despite nobody else EVER truly understanding that except other dear artists." (Sheila Grabarsky, USA)

- "Art has reinforced the necessity of discipline and organization tempered with being kind with oneself." (Kym Barrett, Australia)

- "I make choices to commit to my work. This is how I express myself—what I choose to do for myself. No one has to like what I do; it's up to me to reveal what I see, feel, think, enjoy." (Kay Haneline, USA)

- "Time to paint needs to be scheduled. Only you can make it happen. There will always be multiple demands on your time." (Cynthia J. Lee, USA)

Annie Abdalla, you will recall, is an artist who gets up at 4:45 a.m. every day. Annie is a member of Gampo Abbey, a Tibetan Buddhist monastery in Nova Scotia, Canada where the famous author and Abbot, Pema Chodron, lives. Her story of coming to art later in life began at the point where she'd completed her Master of Fine Arts degree. She'd gone on to teach at Goddard College in Vermont, all the while working on her own art career. At that point in her life, she had just retired from her teaching position, her mother had died, and Annie had no other commitments or caregiving responsibilities. She began a residency at Gampo Abbey. The Abbey offers residencies for those who want to live in the monastic community for a period of nine to twelve months. She writes about these beginnings:

> I came in January 2017 intending to be here for just ten months but decided to stay on. I'd been wanting to do something like this for a while, and as all of the beings that I was directly responsible for had died shortly before, the route was opened for me to do it. I was sixty when I arrived. I knew that I did not want to take life ordination so I stayed at the level of temporary ordination for two-and-a-half years until I gave up my robes in order to take a position here in the leadership team.

Annie sent me her daily schedule, which I include below. I was astonished. Almost every minute is accounted for. After being up at 4:45a.m. she goes to bed relatively early, at 8 p.m. Her day is divided into blocks of time that everyone in the community adheres to. I don't think that most of us would be able to maintain such a routine, nor would our lives allow for it. But it is possible to adjust our schedules to aim for a little more productivity? What sort of artists might we be if we kept to rigorous schedules such as this?

Wake Up	4:45am	
Study/Read/ Write	4:45 – 5:55	In my room with a thermos of tea
	6:00 – 6:40	In the main shrine room with the whole community
House Jobs	6:40 – 7:00	Everyone has a bit of the house to clean. I have two bathrooms to do.
Breakfast	7:00 – 7:20	I don't usually dawdle over breakfast because I want to get some creative time
Art time (many days)	7:20 – 7:45	In my room, or the workshop, or the garden. Somewhere close.
Morning meditation	8:00 – 11:00	In the main shrine room or a smaller shrine room depending on what practice I'm doing that day.
Mind Body Time	11:00 – 12:30pm	Time for exercise, laundry, personal time. I rarely make art in this period because it's important to me to get exercise.
Lunch	12:30 – 1:30	

Service Period	1:30 – 5:00	This is where we do our job function. Since 2019 my job has been managing a larger project that actually requires more than this time slot so I also do some work in the mornings as required.
Evening chants	5:30 - 6:30	In the main shrine room
Medicine Meal	6:30	We don't eat much after midday, just a bowl of soup. In many monasteries they don't eat at all but here we have to do so much physical labour that we need a bit more.
Free time— access		Although I use the internet for my work in the afternoon this is the only period in the day that we have wifi that we can access for personal things.
Bedtime	8:00pm	I like to get into bed by 8 and read some juicy fiction.

Annie fits painting and creativity into her monastic timetable, even if only for twenty-five-thirty minutes at a time. She explains how she came to her particular approach to being an artist:

> I'm a big supporter of little bits of effort repeated regu-
> larly. Kind of like meditation—it doesn't have to be long
> every day but even a small daily, or almost daily practise
> has an impact… I once wrote a master's thesis this way as

well. Back in the late 90s I had taken a few side trips off the path of completing my Masters of Environmental Studies (one side trip was coming to Halifax to do a BFA at Nova Scotia College of Art and Design). Along the way, I hit a bad year of depression where I couldn't read or write much for a full twelve months. But I really wanted to get my thesis finished. I had a rough idea of the chapters, or topics I wanted to cover but no writing yet. My very smart therapist in Halifax could see that I was paralyzed at the prospect of getting this done so she assigned me a task of writing for just 15 minutes per day—no editing, no revising, just writing. Well actually she first said 30 minutes/day but that proved too difficult.

So I took up this routine—I started each day with a question at the top of the page—something like 'what's the relationship between this element of my idea around environmental philosophy and that other issue?'. When you start a MS Word document like this it automatically creates a title for the document from the first line, the question. I'd save the file and I had accomplished my task for the day, a positive feeling. Once there was stuff on paper it was much easier to massage and refine and see what could be cut out. Most of the writing was crap—but at the end of six weeks I had a big folder of material based on these questions that I could fit into the rough chapters. And that's how I wrote my thesis, 15 minutes at a time.

Learning to make art well takes time and effort. Each of us needs to find our own way to that end. It requires focus and effort, setting aside time in the day, believing in ourselves, maybe working like Annie does, in small daily doses.

Part V
Coming to Art
Later in Life:
Opening to
Elderhood

Chapter 20:
Surrender

To live in this world, you must be able to do three things: to love what is mortal; to hold it against your bones knowing your own life depends on it; and, when the time comes to let it go, to let it go.
—Mary Oliver

According to the majority of respondents, the most important benefit of art was not to learn to paint or express themselves or to have a community with whom to show their work, but to *know themselves better*. This was echoed in their responses about the lessons of coming to art which included insights about surrender, patience, authenticity, and learning to live with paradox. And all of these also led to self-knowledge. These unexpected responses led me to consider the possibility that art is, or can be, a training ground for becoming elders in our society or, at least, the elder capacity in all of our psyches. Elders are not simply those who live to an old age, but rather, are those who have maturity and wisdom, who know themselves, who love and appreciate the planet, and whose orientation includes an emphasis on service and care-taking the world, or at least an aspect of it. Older artists are opening up to a new stage of life, turning inward and outward at the same time, and getting to know themselves on a much deeper level.

Through art, we may grow into the role of elder. This role is essential in our society, providing stability and depth, wisdom-keeping, space-holding, and care-taking, and in the words of Bill Plotkin, the very soul of the world."[55]

One aspect of knowing ourselves better is learning to surrender. By the time we reach the age of retirement we've learned to surrender countless times: to our parents; in school; in our work; and most especially if we've had children or had to care for an aging parent or someone who is chronically ill or dying. That understanding of surrender is a crucially important life lesson and in fact is at the heart of all spiritual paths. Surrender, when we're speaking of artists, involves following where our creative work wants to lead us, flowing with it when it gets hard. Surrender is not giving up, it's allowing. It's moving from resistance, or trying to make something happen— trying to control a situation, to letting go. It differs from acceptance in that it's deeper and involves transcending our ego, connecting with our higher selves, our inner wisdom.

As a personal example: When I had the dream of this book, I worked on it for a time, then let it fall away. The idea of the book returned to me, keeping at me in a sense. I resisted. It kept sitting there in my mind waiting, just as my dog stares at me intently when it's time for supper. The book basically stared at me for years. At last, I said, in an exasperated way, 'Okay, I'll do it.' But that wasn't surrender. It wasn't until I actually began to write it and began to enjoy it, learning from it, finding creativity in it, just giving over to the unknown—where the book wanted to go, that I surrendered myself to the process. There's a kind of relief in that, in the idea that I don't have to control everything.

When asked about the life lessons art has taught, US respondent, Carolyn Ellis commented about letting go:

> Because I'm an interior person, a thinker, making abstract art, which is all about interior reality, is a perfect fit for me. Last year, reflecting on how I do my best work when

I hang up my ego and give my subconscious expressive liberty somehow got me thinking about prayer, which is also about hanging up the ego. Then came this completely unlikely leap: I started thinking about my life-long attraction to simplicity. In a flash I suddenly saw that simplicity for me turns out to be a metaphor! It isn't less stuff that I've been after all these years (decades!), it's less of me and more of God that I've been questing after all these years! This was a total revelation in my life. That making abstract art opens me up to personal insights like this continues to totally amaze me.

Making art of any sort requires that we surrender our egos. Stephen Nachmanovitch in *Free Play*, writes,

> I am not in the music business, I am not in the creativity business; I am in the surrender business. Improvisation is acceptance, in a single breath, of both transience and eternity. Surrender means cultivating a comfortable attitude toward not-knowing.[56]

I continue to learn lessons about surrender. One lesson was taught to me by a paintbrush. One summer I took a brush-painting workshop on Vancouver Island on the far west coast of Canada. Our first task was to make our own brush. Our instructor, Lorne Loomer, provided us with red cedar bark that had washed up on a Vancouver Island beach. We were to take the bark outside with us as we searched for a stone that spoke to us. With that stone, we were to beat the red cedar bark into a brush, loosening all the fibres until we had a spindly, feathery-looking object that we were to use as a brush. My bark split into several pieces so I ended up with four brushes of various sizes. Back inside, we dipped our newly made brushes into Chinese ink and then practised making marks on paper. As I stood, bent over my worktable, and played with these brushes, I gradually developed a bodily rhythm, moving back and forth in a sort of rocking motion—over to the ink, then back to the paper, then over to the ink, back and forth, swaying as I painted. I'd never painted in this way before. It was hypnotic and meditative. I disappeared into the work, surrendering to the movement of the brush, letting it speak for itself as it created letters in a secret language.

The 1995 Academy Award nominated film *A Self-Portrait on the Walls*, portrays a similar act of surrender. The American artist and poet Jim Dine teaches us about letting go, surrendering in a direct visual way. Dine was invited to create huge charcoal drawings directly on the walls of the Ludwigsburg Kunstverein Gallery near Stuttgart, Germany. In the film, we are brought right inside his dusty, creative process as we witness Dine's intensity and focus and the difficulties he has to overcome. In eight long days, wearing a mask to filter out the charcoal dust, Dine attacked the drawings with brooms, mops, a screwdriver, aerosol spray, hunks of bread, even Pepsi straight from the can, creating floor-to-ceiling drawings of animals, birds, trees, and a self-portrait—all images that were symbolic to him. For him, the process was exhausting; for the audience, it's exhilarating. We witness the intensity of the procedure, the excitement of the opening, and then we gasp as workers in white overalls come into the gallery with brooms to sweep the work away in a breathtaking display of impermanence. It is an unusual and transitory exhibition in that the drawings remain on the walls for only six weeks before being painted over.[57]

Kym Barrett shares: "The process of making art as it has evolved for me, has taught me the important *art of letting go* … which I think is one of the most valuable lessons in life." It's important to her to be able to let go of that beautiful mark if it doesn't work with the rest of the piece. In life, letting go of long-held concepts/beliefs, personality habits, attachments to people and things.

Letting go is an aspect also found in nature. Think of how nature produces in excess to carry on a species. Female sea turtles, for example, lay between two and six clutches of eggs, each containing sixty-five to 180 eggs. Only 1 out of 1000 hatchlings will survive. This example from nature is instructive for us. We must be willing to throw a lot of artwork away in order to learn to paint, or be willing to let go of a piece and paint over it. Our best work will happen when we surrender to the process, when we let go of expectations, when we let go of ourselves and disappear into the work.

Surrender is a very simple concept but so hard to do. It means giving over control, knowing that we don't know. There's a sense of relief that comes with surrendering. As elder artists, we have likely had to learn about surrender in our lives, in our relationships. Now we learn to surrender to our work, to the mystery, following the work into the unknown.

Chapter 21:
Authenticity

To be nobody but yourself in a world which is doing its best, night and day, to make you everybody else means to fight the hardest battle which any human being can fight; and never stop fighting.
—e.e. cummings

Discovering your authentic self, your true self is an important aspect and significant lesson in coming to art later in life. It is a marker, a signpost on the path to becoming an elder. Remember Phil Cousineau's statement that "a gold thread runs from your soul to your work"? I believe that when we hold that thread, we can't help but be authentic. There's an energy we can feel that lets us know a work of art is honest, authentic, and that it comes from the heart of the artist. It's mysterious but we can feel that authenticity in the same way we can tell when a work is not authentic, when it's created simply to be sold. The soul is missing. It can have all compositional elements in place and still feel as though the artist was on auto-pilot or perhaps distracted with other thoughts while they painted.

The concept of authenticity is not to do with a certain style or way or painting. It's not to do with whether the flinging application of paint is expressive or precise, whether the images are representational or abstract. It's to do with whether the artist is present, and their heart is open. We can feel it if the artist is offering up their focus and their love.

Several of the artists who responded to my questionnaire described authenticity as being one of the significant life lessons they learned from coming to art later in life. American artist Charlotte Cizperle writes about one of the lessons she learned:

> Always be true to yourself. You cannot please everyone and not everyone will like you... or your art... and that is ok. Paint what you like and enjoy. When you are true to yourself, your heart and soul will be reflected in whatever it is you are painting.

A similar sentiment is expressed by Cynthia J. Lee:

> It's important to be true to your personal vision of what you want your painting to be...When I paint from my intuitive impulses, the paintings work for me. My work is original. Only I could make it. Whether or not it is any good is for the viewer to decide.

"A work of art is like a visual form of prayer," writes artist Ian Roberts in his book *Creative Authenticity,16 Principles to Clarify and Deepen Your Artistic Vision*. He goes on to state, "Our response comes from the power of the prayer that contributed to the making of the piece."[58] Perhaps the prayer is our response to the energy of a subject, what the ancient Chinese called qi (pronounced chi). This was the Taoist approach to art. Taoism grew out of various religious and philosophical traditions, including shamanism and nature religions, in ancient China. In the *The Zen Art Book, the Art of Enlightenment,* Stephen Addiss and John Daido Loori, explain the history:

> During its early history, Zen was influenced by the refined practices of Chinese poetry, painting and calligraphy... the *Tao of Painting,* a book written around 500 C.E., is the canon on the art of painting as a spiritual path. By the Song

Dynasty in China (960-1279 C.E.), the Zen arts reached a high stage of development with a novel phenomenon: the emergence of painter-priests and poet-priests who produced art that broke with all standard forms of religious and secular art. This art did not inspire faith or facilitate liturgy or contemplation... It was not used in worship or as a part of prayer. It suggested a new way of seeing and a new way of being that cut to the core of what it meant to be human and fully alive. Zen expresses the ineffable as it helps to transform the way we see ourselves in the world.[59]

David Hinton, a poet and scholar of ancient Chinese poetry, writes more on this idea in his book, *Existence: A Story*. The book in itself is a form of meditation. Hinton tells how in ancient China, language was structured differently from English: there were no nouns, only verbs. He explained:

There was no rigid distinction between noun and verb so things were not linguistically deprived of their 'verb-ness,' their life. Nothing was fixed. Language itself was about impermanence, about movement, about change. Everything was alive. One way the ancient Chinese approached the understanding of existence was to recognize the distinction between heaven and earth, the embodiment of yang (male) and yin (female). We dwell in our everyday lives at the origin place where this vital intermingling of heaven and earth takes place... but we are rarely aware of this wondrous fact. Reinvigorating our awareness of that wonder is one purpose of Chinese landscape painting as a spiritual practice. This explains the primacy of mountain landscape in the tradition, for mountain landscape is where existence itself is most dramatically present as a cosmology of elemental forces, where the intermingling of heaven and earth is most immediately visible.[60]

The ancient Chinese, then, felt they were an integral part of the cosmos, helping to connect heaven and earth. There was no separation. Even their language was alive. It was all one. When they painted, they came from a place of oneness. There was no question of authenticity or being present. The artist was always present and feeling at one with the cosmos. It would be as though painting was another aspect of themselves. While ancient Chinese painters saw no separation between themselves and nature, no separation between themselves and their paintings, what I hope for when I'm in nature, as well as when I'm painting, is to move out of myself, to disappear into the land, into the painting. As our Western beliefs and our very language are about separation, it's not as easy for a Westerner to do that. There are ways though to move out of our human-centeredness and into nature, becoming nature, carrying that energy in our hearts. For example, when I'm painting, I visualize that energy entering me, flowing into my heart, then moving from my heart down my arm and into my hand, being transferred onto my canvas, making a direct connection to the love I want to express. That's how I manage to be present and focused. Interviewed about his recent book of poetry, *The Half-Life of Angels*, Mark Nepo commented:

Being authentic, from the Greek, means "the mark of the hands. So being authentic is how the heart comes into the hands, how inner comes into the world."[61]

David Skillicorn says:

The key for me is authenticity. And perhaps when we get on a little bit, there is less tolerance for BS and more of a sense that time is precious. So perhaps we get a little more real a little more quickly... that is the hope.

It isn't necessary for us to be painter-priests or painter-poets in order to be authentic. What *is* necessary is for us to feel deeply what it is that we're painting. If we can get past our humanness, let go of

ourselves, and feel at one with the world, with nature, feeling no separation, then that is the sense we need to carry into our painting.

Canadian respondent Chris Brown, elaborates on this sense of
authenticity and the connections artists can make when they create
at the soul level:

> Artists often say they make art for themselves, not for
> others. This could simply mean they like to create things
> they personally find entertaining, informative or emotion-
> ally moving. That may be all they intend. But I also hear of
> artists who try to bare their soul in their art. They try to
> plumb the depths of their being and find a way to infuse
> it into their art. They might do it to bring what is inside
> them outside where they can look at it. They might put it
> on public display in such an oblique metaphor that only
> they can see it. As is often the case in literature, a skillful
> artist might include many layers of meaning so that many
> people will enjoy their work. Deep at the bottom, they
> place their inner most essence. But I think some artists
> are not satisfied with this. I think a few expose themselves
> in plain view deliberately. Why do they do this? Is it to
> communicate to another what they find most meaning-
> ful? This other person cannot be anyone. All of the above
> layers are for anyone. This is for a kindred spirit, the one
> who feels what you express at the same deep level from
> which you expressed it. I suspect these people are as rare
> as a true and lifelong friend. But they are out there and
> the only way to find them, to let them learn you are their
> kindred spirit, is to express your deepest, innermost, inti-
> mate self. I think it is this desire to connect with another
> on the deepest possible level that drives a few brave artists
> to bare their souls. I think it has been the driving force in
> the creation of many artists' collectives that developed

unique inner languages they then used among themselves. For the only thing better than baring your soul to another and having them understand and embrace it is for them in turn to bare their soul to you and find you both speak the same deep inner language that you thought belonged to your soul alone. You experience something you have never known before. It is beyond love. I think that is why the bravest of artists make art for themselves. They are making it for that special, as yet unknown, kindred spirit.

In his beautiful articulation, Chris Brown reminds us that whether we're making art for ourselves or for that special unknown kindred spirit, it's important for us to be authentic in our work and create from the deepest part of ourselves.

Chapter 22:
Knowing Ourselves

To live in this world you must be able to do three things: to love what is mortal; to hold it against your bones knowing your own life depends on it; and, when the time comes to let it go, to let it go.
—Mary Oliver

One of the questions I asked artists was, What are some of the benefits of coming to art later in life?' I thought that some might answer it was to keep themselves occupied in retirement. Not so. The most common answer to my question was knowing myself better.' Art "is a lovely and amazing process for exploring yourself, opening up and discovering who you really are," shared David Skillicorn.

We never stop learning if we're open to it, no matter our age. As a young woman, I thought that life basically stopped once you reached about age sixty, that from then on you were just treading water until you died. Of course, as I got to sixty and well past it, I realize that life involves continual growth and development. It's a huge joy to realize that and to understand that as we age we still have something to give back to the world. Mary Morgan, a respondent from the US writes, "The benefit of being an older artist is knowing that I have many stories to tell and that my soul is overflowing with good things."

This concept of getting to know themselves better was also often mentioned by artists when they were responding to my invitation to 'Describe some of the important life lessons art has taught you.' The responses to this invitation were delightfully thoughtful and honest. Some stated that art allowed them to open up to their spirituality. Michela Sorrentino wrote:

> I never have really thought of myself as being a very spiritual person but I discovered that the art making process is in itself quite spiritual. I feel so vulnerable when I make my art. I can feel scared, thrilled, enlightened, frustrated, joyful and even terrified all in a matter of a few hours of painting. I have learned from painting that I will eventually come out the other end of the tunnel no matter how long it is.

Many artists commented that their journeys into becoming artists revealed that they had important things to share. Janet Read, an artist from Canada, shares, "Art taught me that you can work through failure. You can honour the subjective. I learned that I have a voice that can be heard." English artist Anne Armes writes that art taught her, "to be more confident in public as I truly have something to say, and gave me a deeper understanding of who I really am. I have found the real me that I always dreamed of."

The journey into art then can be compared with a pilgrimage, a journey of transformation. Many people know in their deepest selves when they take their first art class that they are searching for something more, more than a hobby, more than a way to pass time in the evening.

A recent study in the *Journal of Clinical Psychiatry* finds a correlation between a sense of meaning and positive physical, mental, and cognitive functioning as we grow older. "Those with meaning in life are happier and healthier than those without it,"[62] indicates senior study author, Dilip V. Jeste. Although a search for meaning may be on our minds at various times in our lives, this study suggests that this search becomes stronger with age:

> After age 60, [as people] retire from their jobs and [may] start to lose their [sense of] identity, they start to develop health issues and some of their friends and family begin to pass away. They start searching for the meaning in life again because the meaning they once had has changed. As we become older, there seems to be a pressing need to know what we should be doing with—and what we should be feeling about—our remaining time. For many people, finding meaning becomes a prerequisite for a happy ending to one's life story. Without it, suggests the study, our declining years and the difficulties they may involve may be dominated by stress and its physical consequence.[63]

Another step in the aging process is letting go. Parker Palmer, author, educator, and activist who focuses on issues in education writes about letting go on his Facebook page of November 8, 2021:

> Twenty years ago, as I began to deal with the realities of aging, I began asking myself two questions: 'What do I need to let go of? What do I want to hang onto?' I still ask the first question, but the second no longer works for me. As life constantly reminds us, we can't hang on to what we love—all of it will take its leave sooner or later, and so will we. So I'm grateful that I was given a different question to ask: 'What do I want to give myself to?' Trying to hang on to what I treasure defies the law of life, and it's a needy, clingy, scarcity-based way of being in the world. But asking what I want to give myself to, directs me toward places where I can find meaning, energy, and a reminder of life's abundance. For me, at least, 'What do I want to give myself to?' is a question that can open up a path with a heart.[64]

A number of questionnaire respondents indicated that through art, they are learning about themselves:

- "I am strong. I am intense. I am capable of the equivalent expressiveness in my painting." (Sheila Grabarsky, USA)

- "I am more than I knew, I am an artist. I can create mysterious things!" (Geri de Gruy, USA)

- "I've learned who I am." (Plum Neasmith, UK)

- "I know what I want to say and express through my work. It absolutely feeds my soul and I have the time to feel that, think about it and write about it. That's the goal of art isn't it, of life, in the end, when all else is blown away through illness, disaster, the death of close ones; to know ourselves better." (Lin Rowsell, Canada)

In addition to the inspiring stories I collected from older artists, I also love the Green Renaissance videos that have a similar goal: to inspire change by sharing the stories of ordinary people who are making a difference. I showed one of these videos titled *A Creative Life* in one of my painting workshops. In the video, four older artists discuss process and their philosophies. Filmed in South Africa and the Faroe Islands, the video features Dawn Garisch, Gina Niederhumer, Ole Jakob Nielsen and Kyoko Kimura Morgan.[65]

Dawn Garisch says, "Creativity is there to help us explore who we are and puts you in touch with what's happening to you so that you live more deeply. I use my art as a way of making sense of my life." As he works, creating a wooden bowl, another of the artists, Ole Jakob Nielsen, says, "the creating process in the workshop is the way of philosophy for me. My hands will communicate my thoughts better than my voice would do." Another artist in the video, Gina Niederhumer, works with textiles and explains: "When you value your own creativity as a huge resource to help you process your own life and anxiety, you come to terms with your life. You come to accept the things that happen to you." Origami is Kyoko Kimura Morgan's art form. In the video, she talks about how she was bullied as a child, which has left a scar in her heart:

And it's the same as paper, once you crease it, it remains. It never goes away. But you can use that line to make another shape. In a way it's necessary to have that crease. So you make use of what lines and points there are and you can create something out of what you have got. Teaching Origami, what I want to create is that awareness that our situation can transform just like paper.

These artists voice the same sentiment stated by many of those who responded: Art is a transformative activity and gives us the opportunity in later years to begin anew.

Chapter 23:
Maturity and Wisdom

You will know that when all's said and done, to become an artist means nothing; whereas to become alive or one's self, means everything.

—e.e. cummings

It doesn't necessarily follow that we gain wisdom and maturity as we grow older. But the artists who responded to my questionnaire and the ones I interviewed indicated that they did see the world differently in their older years. Unlike in Eastern and Indigenous cultures, where elders are honoured for their knowledge and wisdom, in Western society the latter years have generally not been seen as a time of meaningful creative activity; aging has not been viewed as something to look forward to.

However, every one of these older respondents has a more positive view of aging. They tell of embracing the joys of creativity, welcoming the lessons their long lives have taught them, and valuing the knowledge that their last few decades can be not only fulfilling but also full of opportunities to keep growing. They also recognize that they have the opportunity to teach younger people, through example, that the later years aren't just about grey hair, Metamucil, and walkers. There is quality of life there: the joy of learning and growing and keeping alive a curiosity for life.

"Because I'm aging and death is closer and more real than it has ever been," writes Geri de Gruy, "I think I see more clearly, both with my eyes and my heart. I'm willing to be still. I want to take it all in. I want to see the visible and the invisible." Canadian respondent Judy Byer shares:

> Wisdom comes with being older and the ability to see more clearly what is of importance and what things are not that vital for me to have a good and joyful fulfilling life. I no longer feel the need to explain myself and my choices to anyone, I have the freedom to follow the paths that intrigue and excite me.

These types of views are in accordance with a neurocognitive standpoint. In his book, *Successful Aging*, Daniel Levitin writes:

> Wisdom is the ability to see patterns where others don't see them, to extract generalized common points from prior experience and use those to make predictions about what is likely to happen next. Oldsters aren't as fast, perhaps at mental calculations and retrieving names, but they are much better and faster at seeing the big picture. And that comes down to decades of generalization and abstraction. I've come to see aging as not inevitably a period of decline and loss and irrelevance but a period of potentially renewed engagement, energy and meaning-ful activities.[66]

Many of the respondents indicated that becoming artists in later years offered them new ways of engaging with life, new ways of approaching art. The focus is not so much on achieving and selling as it would have been when they were younger; age and maturity have caused a shift in emphasis. They acknowledge that there is a business side of art, the need to get the work out into the world, to sell it, but for many, their main focus has shifted. They're not so interested in the marketing side of art making; art has become more of an inward practice.

This has been my experience too. While I love making art and still maintain a passion for it, my focus has shifted and I'm just as interested in sharing my love of art with others through teaching, conducting workshops, and writing about it. I'm aiming to help my students become better artists, but beyond that, I want to help them learn about themselves through their own art, to make a deeper connection to themselves, and in turn to the rest of the world, particularly the land.

One of the artists who reported a shift in focus is Annie Abdalla. She had this to say about her experience:

> In recent years my aspirations and intentions have shifted some. I still have some work in a couple of galleries here in Nova Scotia, but I'm growing less interested in making 'art to sell' and more interested in art making as a practice and sharing that practice with others. Right from the get-go I have been fascinated in how the actual making can change consciousness. I suppose I was pulled in a few different directions over the years, thinking that making art to exhibit and sell would satisfy my curiosity about what it feels like to be an artist. I was clearly stuck on what feels like old-fashioned ideas from a modernist history. I believe that the whole world of art is now discarding those ideas of the great artist in a garret. I'm excited to see a greater emergence of the idea of art making as a way of knowing the world, of figuring things out personally, and as a way to share ideas with others.

All of these observations point to the fact that with maturity comes a deeper understanding of what's important in our lives.

Chapter 24:
Love and Care for the World

And what we need is a great, powerful, tremulous falling back in love with our old, ancient, primordial Beloved, which is the Earth herself.
—Martin Shaw

When asked what important life lessons art has taught them, artists responded most frequently that art helped them know themselves better. The second most frequent life lesson they acquired was gratitude for and appreciation of the world around them:

- "[Art taught me] to look and appreciate more. To see beauty in so many fleeting things (I believe in the restorative power of beauty). To experience the world more intensely, which is a source of joy." (Alethea Eriksson, Switzerland)

- "Art has taught me to fully appreciate nature and how the seasons change throughout the year, something I had not appreciated when working.... I have become a more accurate and active observer. Painting has given me a sense of stillness and quiet; it has made me slow down and think about my part in the universe." (Hilary Dron, UK)

- "Art has fundamentally changed the way I look at the world around me." (Susan Cartwright, Canada)

- "Art has given me a sense of awe." (Dorothy Doherty, Canada)

It seems like such a simple concept, being grateful, but in the past twenty years there has been increased scholarly attention on the dimensions of this attitude. Gratefulness has become a subject of scientific research and seems to be part of a movement. In his book *"Thanks!: How the New Science of Gratitude Can Make You Happier,"* psychologist Robert Emmons shows that those who practise gratitude tend to be more creative, bounce back more quickly from adversity, have a stronger immune system and even a longer life.[67]

Brother David Steindl-Rast explains, "that every moment is a 'given moment.' It's a gift." Brother David is an American Benedictine monk, author and lecturer, and co-founder of the website, gratefulness. org who goes on to say, "You haven't earned that gift of the present moment or brought it about. And you have no way of assuring there will be another moment given to you."[68] As such, we should consider each moment as precious and a great opportunity.

I've always had an appreciation for nature, even as a child, and painting has made me even more appreciative of nature because it involves being present in the moment, being aware, seeing details. We can become totally absorbed in the way clouds cast shadows on the land on a sunny day, the relationship of one object to another, or the number of colours there are in tree bark or in the rocks on the ground. My eyes might fall in love, say, with the way the purplish shadow of a tall tree falls across the yellow-green of a patch of grass in early spring. This awareness made me more present to the details, the beauty all around me and increased my sense of gratitude for that. Now I paint non-objectively, moving beyond a representation of the world around me, appreciating the energy in a landscape as I search for the soul or spirit of the land.

This sense of deep connection and appreciation motivates me to act on behalf of the Earth—to protect the quiet and beautiful spaces that inspire me. "Silence is on the verge of extinction," [69] explains acoustic ecologist Gordon Hempton. He circles the globe recording the sound of quiet places in an effort to save them. In an *On Being* podcast interview in May 2012, about his book, *One Square Inch of Silence, One Man's Quest to Preserve Quiet,* Hempton declares that "silence is so endangered, we even need another word for it. Places in nature that never have any noise pollution are already gone. When you save quiet, you actually wind up saving everything else, too."[70] The World Health Organization realizes that silence is a precious commodity that is fast disappearing. In 1999, they developed guidelines on the topic of noise. reporting noise as being the second largest environmental cause of health problems.[71]

In a very noisy world, some people are afraid of silence. There is actually a term for this sort of fear: sedatephobia. Perhaps there is a fear of visual silence in art as well.

Most participants have too much going on: too many small shapes, too much texture, extremes of colour, too many lines, too much, too much. One thing I suggest often as I walk around the classroom working with students individually, is to make bigger, quieter shapes. These are large areas, painted smoothly, that seem boring with no texture. Don't be afraid of them. They are the strong support shapes that allow the other areas to sing. They can't be heard if every single part of the painting is shouting.

The Irish author Colm Toibin was interviewed on CBC radio in archived interview about his 2012 novel, *The Testament of Mary.* Among other topics, he spoke of the process of writing and the importance of silence. The spaces between the words, he said, are more important than the words themselves.[72]

Similarly in music, silence is crucial. There's a wonderful article on the website, *All About Jazz,* concerning the role of silence in jazz:

The best musicians use silence. Great artists have impeccable technique, but as part of this they also know how to use silence. Accomplished composers don't take all their best ideas and muddy the listener's experience by rattling on and on. These artists know how to communicate their ideas clearly. Listen to the space between the phrases. Listen to how one instrument comes forward when others move into the background. Listen to how the solos fill the listener's experience because there's not competition from other voices. Listen to how silence is used as a color, and not simply as the lifeless backdrop of compositions. Silence, when used effectively, is a color. It's one of the colors on a composer's palette.[73]

Music inherently depends on silence. There's a post on the *Classic FM* blog about the importance of silence in classical music, where the author discusses Mahler's Symphony No. 9, among others:

The final passage of the final movement, Mahler's farewell to the world (he was diagnosed with terminal heart disease as he composed it), also contains some of the most poignant silence imaginable. The final notes are marked 'esterbend' (dying away), so it's almost impossible to tell when the silence actually begins but it's loaded with such incredible thematic weight that it becomes weirdly deafening. You strain so hard to hear something that, ultimately, you just can't.[74]

While many poets, writers, and musicians recognize the importance of silence in their work, I find that much contemporary art is noisy. A few years ago, I went to an art. exhibition called *60 Painters*. The show was described as "the most ambitious overview of contemporary Canadian painting in recent memory." It included emerging as well as established artists from across Canada. While there were definitely some incredible paintings in the exhibition, I found most to be visually overwhelming; the canvases were covered top to bottom with activity—lines, marks, texture. Every corner was painted. Every square inch. Each painting was visually shouting, as teenagers would when trying to vie for attention with the loudest voice. Paintings need a quiet space to balance the louder elements. As the musician, Passenger sings, "All I need's a whisper in a world that only shouts."[75]

In the fall of 2012, the Menil Collection in Houston—which houses the Rothko Chapel—had an exhibition of selected paintings from its collection entitled *Silence*. The catalogue stated:

> Silence is a powerful force. It can produce profound emotions or conjure startling sensory experiences, and it seems inextricably linked to the passage of time. A prerequisite for contemplative thought, silence has become a scarce commodity in today's media-saturated world. This is a little-examined subject in modern and contemporary art.[76]

In the workshops I teach, I find that over-expressiveness, that need to fill every corner of a canvas to be one of the most common problems with paintings. Most participants have too much going on: too many small shapes, too much texture, extremes of colour, too many lines, too much, too much. One thing I suggest often as I walk around the classroom working with students individually, is to make big, quiet shapes. Aim for simplicity, allowing room to breathe. These are large areas, painted smoothly, that seem boring with no texture. Don't be afraid of them. They are the strong support shapes that allow the other areas to sing. They can't be heard if every single part of the painting is shouting. I teach this concept in my painting classes as we travel to remote and quiet places.

Canadian artist Gaye Oxford, a participant in my workshops, says that travel to these remote places "invites wild and soul to dance together" and then to carry that dance into painting. Art requires presence and paying attention and this creates connection As US respondent Ruth Andre says, "I've developed an appreciation of beauty and awareness of the world around me in a more conscious way."

As we connect with and appreciate the spirit or soul of the land, it is my hope that older artists who are called to care for this world, will fall back in love with our beautiful, ancient Earth, and use their voices and their influence to try to preserve nature and quiet places.

Chapter 25:
Eldering

True elders can hear the Earth whispering her guidance.
Especially at this time of great crisis and transition,
it is the Earth's guidance that we most need.
—Bill Plotkin

Eldering is a verb, implying activity and movement. It implies continued learning and developing of our inner consciousness. Our art practice can help us do that inner work.

Becoming an artist is not a smooth path. There are rocks to climb over, tree roots that can trip us up, demons in the shadows. What happens along that bumpy path is that we are offered the gift of changing and growing. We learn patience with ourselves, we open to our vulnerabilities, we gain confidence, and we discover our courage and independent spirits, as we let go of old hurts and wounds. In the very act of creating art, we find we can occasionally touch the inner source, the place where everything and everyone are connected. This is a beautiful and powerful place to be, better than any accolades, awards, grants or gallery exhibitions. This is the work of eldering. We don't get to that place just by being old. We have to do the inner work.

As of 2020 , there were an estimated 727 million people aged sixty-five years or over worldwide. This number is projected to more than double by 2050, reaching over 1.5 billion persons. In Canada, in 2022, the population age sixty-five or older numbered 7,329,910, or 18.8% of the population. In the US, the population age 65 and older numbered 54.1 million in 2019 (the most recent year for which data are available). They represented 16 percent of the population, more than one in every seven Americans. The 65-and-older population in the US grew by over a third during the past decade, and by 3.2 percent from 2018 to 2019. The sheer numbers are forcing us to have another look at old age.

"Ageism is the latest acceptable prejudice," says Ashton Applewhite, activist and author in her 2017 TED talk. She goes on to say it's a separation from time, dividing our lives into separate segments that aren't united. "It's a prejudice," Applewhite says, "against our own future selves."[77]

We have to come to terms with those parts of ourselves that will grow old, with being diminished in power and physical appeal. Some keep clinging to youth by getting bodies surgically changed, faces altered. We could buy into society's stereotypes or we could accept that the diminishment of our bodies is the time to turn inward and expand our consciousness. Being an elder is an opportunity to move into a new inward-looking chapter of our lives. Because this generation of Baby Boomers is still large, and living so long, our generation is just beginning to define what this new chapter will be.

David Suzuki, eighty-seven year-old Canadian academic, a long-time science broadcaster and environmental activist, writes about elders on his website, suzukielders.org:

> We treat elders like a pain in the neck, …just get the hell out of the way, they don't even text message, they don't know how to use the bank any more. But they have something no other group in society has. They've lived an entire lifetime. They've had an entire experience. They have lived their lives, they've made a helluva

lotta mistakes, they have had a few successes. They have learned important lessons."[78]

Suzuki's enthusiasm is infectious. He urges older people to get involved. Get involved not just in community drop-in centres to play bingo or cards or have social evenings, not just to take a class on managing your finances in old age, but to get involved in life, in teaching young people about what you've learned in this life. His advice to elders is straight-forward and insistent:

> So I say to elders, get off the golf course, get off the couch, get on with the most important part of your life. You owe it to the young people now to tell them what the hell you've learned.[79]

Neuroscientist Daniel Levitin's advice to elders is similar. In his January 2020 interview, "The Keys to Aging Well" for *Daily Good*, a portal that shares inspiring quotations and news, he states that his number one recommendation for aging successfully is 'don't retire.' He reports that in a conversation he'd recently had with Jane Goodall, she said something similar: "Don't retire. Keep going… If you do retire, make sure you have something equally compelling that will engage you. That could be philanthropy, it could be education."[80]

In the book *From Age-ing to Sage-ing: A Revolutionary Approach to Growing Older*, Rabbi Zalman Schacter-Shalomi indicates that we have historical precedent of the power of being an elder:

> Throughout most of history, elders occupied honoured roles in society as sages and seers, leaders and judges, guardians of the traditions, and instructors of the young. They were revered as gurus, shamans, wise old men and women who helped guide the social order and who initiated spiritual seekers into the mysteries of inner space.[81]

Rabbi Zalman claims that the loss of empowerment in the elderly came about as a result of the Industrial Revolution which emphasized technology, an area that was outside the knowledge of most seniors. They tended to feel overwhelmed by advanced technology and lost their power and status as elders in society. Now we see this lack of status and power as normal old age.[82]

Rabbi Zalman emphasizes that we don't automatically become elders simply by living to old age. We must undertake the inner work that leads gradually to expanded consciousness. He calls that 'eldering.' An active verb. It suggests movement, the ongoing learning and developing process toward an inner awareness of what being an elder can be.[83]

Author Velma Wallis shares story about elders that I love, entitled *Two Old Women*.[84] This story is an Athabascan Indian legend that was passed orally from mothers to daughters for generations in the upper Yukon River Valley in Alaska. Even in those times it seems, elders had to earn respect. The tribe had looked after two old negative, complaining women as the tribe had moved from place to place in search of food in the merciless northern landscape. One brutally cold winter, in a time of terrible famine, the chief thought that one way to help the tribe was to reduce the number of mouths to feed. He decided to leave the old women behind. A grandson of one of the women gave them an axe and lots of leather strips they could use for sewing. Shocked, hurt and betrayed, the old women decided that if they were going to die that they may as well die trying. Their incentive for life quickly came back. They remembered all the skills they had learned as young women, made snowshoes, and started a journey to a campsite that they remembered that had an abundance of fish and wildlife. With steely determination, they completed this long journey. When they finally arrived, they built a shelter, caught and smoked fish, and stored them in the earth. Proud of their accomplishments, they shared stories with each other over their campfire each night. After many more weeks had passed, the tribe returned to this area of the river, still starving. They were shocked that the old women were still alive. When they could finally let go of their anger, the old women forgave the tribe and shared their food, earning at last, the respect of the tribe. This story illustrates that becoming an elder involves more than growing older. It involves continuing to grow and learn, being engaged in the world and contributing as you are able. It also suggests that passing on their knowledge to the next generation was an important contribution these two old women could have given.

Depth psychologist Bill Plotkin wrote that elders are those who have worked to discover their souls, their places in the world, the jobs they were called here to do, and beyond that to feel responsibility for "the care of the soul of the world." Plotkin believes that "above and beyond social-vocational roles, each person has a unique ecological role, a role she was *born* for, a singular way he can serve and nurture the web of life."[85]

I believe that we open up to this deep caring as we move through life, especially if we are fortunate enough to become grandparents. If we haven't cared for the state of the earth before then, it can become of prime importance when we have grandchildren and consider what we want to pass on to them. "The difference between caring for the world and caring for the soul of the world is the difference between ecology and spiritual ecology... When our consciousness focuses on the soul of the world, we see the world as something that is sacred."[86]

Thich Nhat Hanh, the Vietnamese Buddhist monk, demonstrated his reverence for the Earth in the way he walked. He seemed to meditate with his feet, walking extremely slowly, mindfully aware that with each careful step he was walking on the skin of the sacred Earth. If we try to think in this way, we'll find that we are walking in a whole different way.

Thanks to Thich Nhat Hahn as well as the consciousness movement of the 'sixties, 'seventies and 'eighties, the teachings of shamanism, Tibetan Buddhism, and Sufism became available to Western culture. Our pathway to expanded consciousness became available to us through yoga, meditation, and contemplative Christianity among other practices. The pieces are in place for older people to develop into elders. Unlike the young, who are usually focused on raising families and working on their careers, we seniors have the time for contemplation, time to develop a wider focus on the world, to connect with the Earth in a profound way, to see the interconnection of all things. Thich Nhat Hanh, in describing the interconnection among all things, said, "we inter-are."[87]

By the time we older artists begin to paint in a serious way, life has taught us how to hold paradox, to reconcile opposites. As I was writing this book, a dear and long-time friend unexpectedly died of a massive heart attack while parking his car one evening. A week later, in the full moon of a late fall morning, my fourth grandchild was born. I held great grief and intense joy simultaneously. A few weeks later, I learned a friend was sitting one cold winter night with overwhelming grief and anger in a police station in Illinois as his two teenage daughters tearfully and painfully told the officer about their traumatic sexual assault. As my friend sat there holding anger and pain, an old man shuffled in to the station laden with winter coats for the collection box. Then a woman came in and asked for help carrying in all the coats she had in the trunk of her car that she'd collected from her friends. And then another person came in. And another. Sitting there, his heart was full of both the deep pain and anger over his daughters' assaults and the joy of witnessing the outpouring of love people were showing to others in need. We learn to hold paradox.

Creating any form of art involves holding opposites because art is a synthesis of head and heart. If only our head is involved in our artwork, the work ends up as an intellectual exercise. This can occur if the purpose of our installation or painting is to angrily critique some aspect of life or express an obscure intellectual idea. That makes it hard for others to connect with the work, and they may end up having to read the treatise on the wall beside the art piece in order to understand it. On the other, if only our heart is involved in our work, self-expression isn't balanced with concepts or meaning. It would be like sitting down at the piano making noise, expecting to play like Oscar Peterson but with no training or skill. It's necessary to first of all have the skill, to learn the craft. And within that container it's necessary to hold the balance of head and heart.

In art, we are in effect, creating the world. The world contains opposites—dark and light; warm and cool; large shapes, small shapes; loud areas, quiet spaces—and, as in life, it's the interplay of opposites that come together creating wholeness in the painting. With each painting we are creating the world, or a small world within the world. Our work then must be made up of opposites coming together: warm, cool; light, dark; loud, quiet. A painting, if successful, holds the balance of life.

David Hinton writes about a form of painting called Ch'an paint-ing, which is related to a form of Buddhism:

> The main aspiration of Chinese spiritual practice was to get past the constructed ego and act *with* and *as* nature. The goal of painting Ch'an was to let the energy that animates the tree and the river also guide your brush. *Wu*-wei, which literally means 'not acting,' was an ideal state. It doesn't refer to doing nothing; it refers to leaving behind that alienated, calculating version of yourself. When a painter integrates him or herself with the cosmos, it's as though the power that uplifted the real mountains is at work on the paper. Actually, it's not 'as though' the same power is at work; it *is* the same power.[88]

Just as in Ch'an paintings, I believe the job of an artist is to integrate him- or herself with the cosmos, with the opposites that exist in the world. Their job is first to learn the necessary skills of their craft and then to let go of the self and become one with the world.

According to Daniel Levitin, older people are able to see patterns more clearly than young people.[89] When we develop and expand our consciousness, we can see the interrelationships between disparate things, between all things, between ideas past and present, between each of us, between us and the world around us. We can see the beauty of the whole and through that, gratitude and more than that, joy. It's important to find our own way to take that knowledge out into the world, whether it be by teaching our grandchildren appreciation for the Earth, creating art, or finding ways to help other older folks become elders.

John Robinson is helping older people become elders through his books on aging. I met John, author of the book *The Three Secrets of Aging*, on a pilgrimage to India in 2005. In doing research on elders for this book, I discovered two books John had written and happily reconnected with him. In *The Three Secrets of Aging*, he writes of his intense initiation into becoming an elder. As in a shaman's initiation, Robinson has gone through intense life-threatening physical and life-altering challenges which he describes in his book. And like a shaman, he has come through them with deep spiritual wisdom and healing powers. He believes, as I do, that our final stage of life is the most important one, that of becoming an elder. Elderhood is not for everyone, Robinson states. The possibility of entering this stage of life is available to everyone, but it only happens if we do the work, if we rise to meet the call.

Robinson describes three stages of elderhood, similar to those described by Plotkin.[90] The first is becoming aware of aging, aware of inevitable death. This can happen through retirement, a sudden cancer diagnosis, loss of a spouse, a moment of sudden insight. Or it can happen gradually—with aching knees, the inability to easily get up from the floor, or the experience of seeing photos of ourselves with double chins and sagging bodies. This is the initiation stage: recognition. The second stage, as described by John Robinson, Rabbi Zalman, and Bill Plotkin is doing the inner work to become an elder. This is the difficult work of inner development, looking at our lives, accepting the path we've taken, the choices we've made and those we haven't, forgiving the hurts imposed by others and forgiving ourselves for how we've hurt others.[91]

Art can be a powerful vehicle for this type of self-discovery as art therapy has surely proven. Those who come to art later in life are eldering—doing the inner work of learning about themselves, expanding their consciousness through the practice of art. We're not simply learning the techniques, although that is definitely part of the process, but we are also experiencing the inner growth of our consciousness through that process, that deeper learning about ourselves. Lynn Alker reflects:

> I see things, people, life differently, more intuitively and with a fragility I didn't notice before. Some of my art has surprised and shocked me with its raw emotion and guttural images. As if I am shedding and purging unpleasant parts of myself or my history.

Getting to know themselves was the answer most people gave when asked both about the benefits of coming to art later in life, as well as the most important life lesson they learned in the process. Most people probably didn't sign up for their first art class with that in mind, but that's one of the benefits of coming to art. It's a spiritual practice, ever so slowly opening us up to greater self-awareness, to elderhood.

There's a third stage of elderhood surpassing the awareness of our aging process and the acceptance of dying, a stage beyond the work of inner development. Robinson describes it as finding heaven on earth where we become appreciative of everything about life.[92] Rabbi Zalman takes this step into action, and describes an elder as 'holding the field' for community. He writes:

> By holding the field—by recognizing our inherent potential, by desiring the fullest expression of our unique gifts and by empowering us to act through an infusion of loving wisdom, we receive a spark, comparable to a spiritual battery jump, that enables us to embrace our destiny and to move courageously into the future.[93]

Authors writing about elders make similar points about the step beyond the work of inner development. Rabbi Zalman writes, "As an integral part of their mission to build the future, elders need to foster a renewed relationship with our devastated planet Earth."[94] Bill Plotkin states, "elders are those who… feel responsibility for the care of the soul of the world."[95] As elders and as artists, we can display our care for the soul of the world through our art and the healing that it brings to ourselves as well as the Earth.

Chapter 26:
Late Blooming

It's never too late to be what you might have been.
—George Eliot

There is a timing for things. It isn't a mistake or a sign of weakness when a person waits until later in life to become an artist. It's just that the time hasn't been right for them to do so any earlier. Like late-blooming plants, they've weathered the heat, the winds, and the fierce summer storms and now, the autumn is their time.

In her audio book, *The Late Bloomer: Myths and Stories of the Wise Woman Archetype*, Clarissa Pinkola Estes describes how this timing is different for everyone: "The Late Bloomer is the one at the verge of tipping forward into her creative powers...her great talent yet untapped...touchingly wondrous yet wounded or held back by fate in some way."[96] Why do some of us bloom late? That's just the way it is. Not everything blooms at the same time.

Like the saguaro cactus that only blooms after thirty-five years, I bloomed late too, attending art school in my late forties. It was the right time for me to go through that experience. Until then, I was busy focusing on family and work which was right for me at the time. Canadian respondent Otto Ahlers expressed a similar sentiment:

The passion I experience—especially painting in the abstract—is some of the deepest joy I have ever known. It might have been fun to experience this earlier, but I've had a life before art of playing and competing in sport and loving my career that I wouldn't trade.

"Some things in life take living long enough to create" says Molly Peacock in an interview in AARP bulletin review about her book, *The Paper Garden.* [97] I couldn't agree more. Some of us need maturity in order to flower. I needed maturity and confidence to handle the times when I was flattened by a critique of my work or by lack of interest in it from the teachers. I wouldn't have been strong enough to handle that in my twenties.

I know that I am blooming at exactly the right age. All of my life experiences—my family, my friends, my studies, the books I've read, my travels, the joys and heartbreaks in life, and the way I've reacted to them—have molded me into the person I am today and therefore have influenced the way I express myself in my art.

As older artists, we've taken the journey to get to this stage of our lives and have overcome challenges along the way. We've overcome our fears of not being taken seriously as we've changed our identities to that of artists, learning to acknowledge and appreciate ourselves as we move into a time in our lives when we finally have the freedom of retirement. Our time is open-ended but also limited. We know there's an ending ahead. Such knowledge makes time more precious and as artists, we don't want to waste it. Art is not just a pastime, something to fill our days in retirement. As so many of the artists who responded to my questionnaire write, art opens up a door unexpectedly into a whole new stage of life, a spiritual path. This is a path toward becoming an elder. As we walk through the door of elderhood, we take on the responsibility of that role, a role that recognizes the oneness of life, that we are all connected and each is a reflection of the whole.

We bring a richness to our art when we arrive later in life after we have done the work—a depth that wasn't accessible to us when we were young. No one asks why some flowers bloom in the autumn. We're just grateful that they do.

Acknowledgements

First of all, thanks to the spirit of the book itself for giving me the dream, and for staying with me, pestering me to keep working on it, following me, and never leaving me alone. I wouldn't have believed that such a thing could happen. And I never imagined that I'd thank you. But I am. Now it's time to give you wings.

Thank you to each of the 138 artists who responded to my questionnaire and allowed me to share their words and their stories and for their extreme patience while I wrote this book. I am very grateful for your willingness to trust me with your stories.

I'm so grateful to Marjorie Anderson who was my early editor. She encouraged me and nudged me along when I lost energy and confidence.

Thanks my three beautiful friends who offered to read my manuscript and give me helpful and encouraging feedback: Sherry Glanville, Catherine Randall, and Anita Berkis.

Big hugs and thanks to Kim Garcia for her advice, support and encouragement.

Thanks to John Robinson for his suggestions and advice.

Big thanks to Jake Babad who helped me greatly with legal advice.

Thanks to my beloved dog Hue, for his silent and steady presence on my journey.

Thanks to all of the students who have attended my classes over the years and those who have come with me on some awe-inspiring adventures.

The biggest thanks of all go to my daughter, Jen Mason and my son, Andrew Mason for helping me pull this book together. Thanks to Andrew for my gorgeous book cover, his website design and his creative back cover writing. And thanks to Jen for her help designing the questionnaire, for teaching me how to deal with the data, and then for her brilliant editing, restructuring and careful proofreading skills, encouraging me to stick with it. Thanks to both of you for helping create a work of art. I am beyond grateful.

Blessings to my four beautiful grandchildren: Kya, Noah, Emmett and Henry. You are a gift and a joy.

About the Author

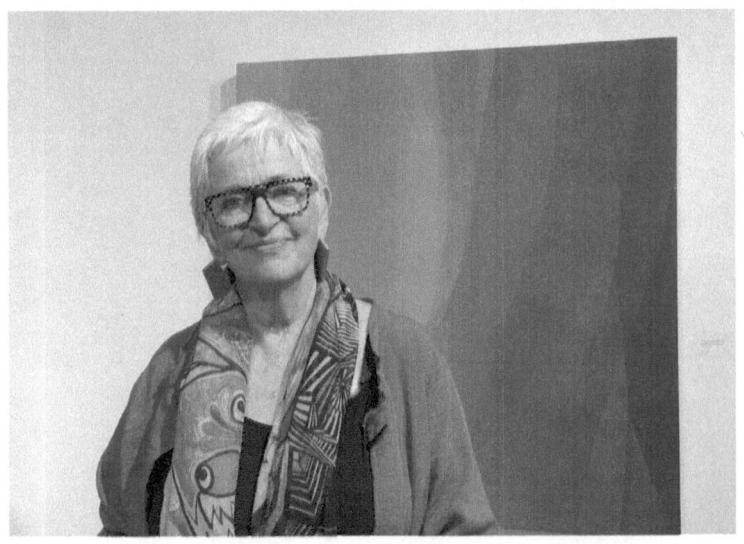

Janice Mason Steeves has been a professional visual artist for forty years and currently shows her work in Canadian galleries. Her work is in private, public, and corporate collections in Canada, the USA, the UK, Italy and Sweden. She has taught painting classes for thirteen years and has developed a program called "Workshops in Wild Places," in which she takes small groups of artists for painting workshops in remote locations in the world. The main purpose of these workshops is to inspire artists to deepen their connection to the land, to fall back in love with the Earth, and to paint from that place of connection.

The author lives in a house that is nestled in the woods outside of Toronto.

Notes

[1] Sara Lawrence-Lightfoot, *The Third Chapter: Passion, Risk and Adventure in the 25 years after 50.*

[2] Plotkin, "Care of the Soul of the World", *Spiritual Ecology: The Cry of the Earth* (Point Reyes Station: The Golden Sufi Center, 2013), 211.

[3] Phil Cousineau, Stoking the Creative Fires: 9 Ways to Rekindle Passion and Imagination (Conari Press, 2008), 37.

[4] Cousineau, *Stoking*, 35.

[5] Cousineau, *Stoking*, 37.

[6] Cousineau, *Stoking*, 33.

[7] Daniel J. Levitin, *Successful Aging: A Neuroscientist Explores the Power and Potential of Our Lives* (Penguin) 2020, xxvii.

[8] Douglas Abrams, *The Book Of Joy: Lasting Happiness in a Changing World,* (Viking, 2016), 7.

[9] Abrams, *Book of Joy*, 293.

[10] Abrams, *Book of Joy*, 303.

[11] Amy Jo Ehman, *Thelma: A Life in Pictures,* (MacIntyre Purcell Publishing Inc., 2020), 59.

[12] Ehman, *Thelma*, 146.

[13] Lillian Michiko Blakey, email, November 2021.

[14] Pico Iyer, "Why We Travel", 2000, https://www.picoiyerjourneys.com

[15] Larry Alton, '5 Scientifically Proven Health Benefits of Traveling Abroad', 2017, https://nbcnews.com.

[16] Lea Lane, Physical Activity Guideline Advisory Committee: *Forbes Magazine*, 2015 https://www.forbes.com/sites/lealane/2015/03/06/yes-travel-is-extraordinarily-good-for-you-experts-show-how-and-why/?sh=4a87caf82642

[17] Brent Crane, "For a More Creative Brain, Travel", *The Atlantic*, March, 2015.https://www.theatlantic.com/health/archive/2015/03/for-a-more-creative-brain-travel/388135/

[18] Girija Kaimal, Kendra Ray & Juan Muniz (2016) Reduction of Cortisol Levels and Participants' Responses Following Art Making, *Art Therapy*, 33:2, 74-80, DOI: 10.1080/07421656.2016.1166832

[19] Jamie Katz, "Unleash Your Inner Genius", *AARP Magazine*, 2010. https://www.aarp.org

[20] Samantha Melamed, "At 100, Frieda Lefeber Gets Her First Gallery Show", *Philadelphia Inquirer*, 2015.

[21] Molly Peacock, "Some Art Required Living Long", *AARP Bulletin*, 2011. https://wwwaarp.org.

[22] Peacock, *AARP Bulletin*.

[23] Amanda Palmer, "Vincent Van Gogh oh Fear, Taking Risks and How Making Inspired Mistakes Moves Us Forward", *The Marginalian*, 2015. https://www.the marginalian.org.

[24] Palmer, *The Marginalian*.

[25] Kathy Stinson, email, 2022.

[26] E.L. Doctorow, ed. George Plimpton, "Writers at Work: The Paris Review Interviews", *The Paris Review*, 1963

[27] Mary Oliver, "The Journey", *No Voyage and Other Poems*, (Houghton Mifflin, 1965).

[28] Jim Dine, "Meet the Artist Jim Dine": *TateShots*, 2009.

[29] Cousineau, *Stoking*, 67.

[30] Cousineau, *Stoking*, 70.

[31] Mary Oliver, "Of Power and Time", *Blue Pastures*, (Harcourt Inc. 1995), 7.

[32] Linda Grasso, *Equal Under the Sky: Georgia O'Keeffe and Twentieth-Century Feminism* (University of New Mexico Press, 2019) 195.

[33] David Whyte, "Vulnerability", *The Marginalian,* April 2016. https://www.the marginalian.org.

[34] Bronnie Ware, *The Top Five Regrets of the Dying* (Hay House, 2011), 37.

[35] Stephen Nachmanovitch, *Free Play: Improvisation in Life and Art* (Tarcher/ Putnam, 1990), 21.

[36] Kent Nerburn, *Dancing with the Gods: Reflections in Life and Art* (Canongate Books, 2018), 30.

[37] Kenny Werner, *Effortless Mastery: Liberating the Musician Within* (Kenny Werner, 2011), 49.

[38] Nachmanovitch, *Free Play,* 81.

[39] Alan Bamburger, "Reasons to Make Art in a Series", https://www.artbusiness.com.

[40] Viggo Mortensen and Pilar Perez ed., *Strange Familiar: The Work of Georg Gudni,* (Perceval Press, 2005), 17.

[41] Matthew Fox, *Creativity: Where the Divine and Human Meet* (Tarcher, 2002), 72.

[42] Elizabeth Gilbert, "Your Elusive Creative Genius", *TED talks,* February, 2009.

[43] Angeles Arrien, *The Nine Muses* (Tarcher, 2002), 6.

[44] Mihaly Csikszentmihalyi, *Flow: The Psychology of Optimal Experience* (HarperCollins, 2008).

[45] Adrian Searle, "The Devil Inside", *The Guardian,* January, 2004.

[46] Science Daily, "This Is Your Brain on Jazz" *Science News,* February, 2008.

[47] Sandra Ingerman, *Shamanic Journeying: A Beginner's Guide* (Sounds True, 2021), 4.

[48] John Kabat-Zinn, https//:www.mindful.org.

[49] Mary Lance, *Agnes Martin: With My Back to the World,* (New Deal Films, 2003).

[50] Seth Mydans, "Thich Nhat Hahn on Life, War and Happiness", *New York Times*, https://www.nytimes.com/2022/01/22/world/asia/thich-nhat-hanh-quotes.html

[51] Nachmanovitch, *Free Play*, 48.

[52] Sydney Pollack, *Sketches of Frank Gehry*, Documentary, 2006.

[53] Stephen Hawkings, "An Imperfect Universe", YouTube, 2011 (no longer available).

[54] Eric Maisel, *Coaching the Artist Within: Advice for Writers, Actors, Visual Artists and Musicians* (New World Library, 2005), 140.

[55] Plotkin, Spiritual Ecology, 214

[56] Nachmanovitch, *Free Play*, 21.

[57] Richard Stilwell, *Jim Dine: A Self-Portrait On the Walls* (University of California Extension Center for Media and Independent Learning,1995).

[58] Ian Roberts, *Creative Authenticity: 16 Principles to Clarify and Deepen Your Artistic Vision*, (Atelier Saint-Luc Press, 2004), 29

[59] Stephen Addiss and John Daido Loori, *The Zen Art Book: The Art of Enlightenment* (Shambhala, 2009), 2.

[60] David Hinton, *Existence: A Story* (Shambhala, 2016), 12

[61] Tami Simon, "Mark Nepo", *Insights at the Edge* podcast, *Sounds True* (2023) https://www.dailygood.org/story/3126/mark-nepo-the-half-life-of-angels-tami-simon/

[62] Robby Berman, "Finding life's meaning can keep us healthy as we age", *Medical News Today*, (2019), https www.medicalnewstoday.com/articles/327345.

[63] Dilip V. Jeste, Meaning in Life and its Relationship with Physical, Mental, and Cognitive Functioning: A Study of 1,042 Community-Dwelling Adults across the Lifespan *Journal of Clinical Psychiatry*. 2019 Dec 10.

[64] Parker Palmer, Facebook Post, November 8, 2021.

[65] "A Creative Life-Art is a Guarantee to Sanity", *Green Renaissance*, YouTube https://www.youtube.com/watch?v=Hp0KoXh6Rnc.

[66] Daniel Levitin, *Successful Aging: A Neuroscientist Explores the Power and Potential of Our Lives* (Penguin, 2020), 37.

[67] Robert Eammons, *Thanks! How the Science of Gratitude Can Make You Happier,* (Boston: Houghton Mifflin, 2007). 13.

[68] Brother David Steindl-Rast, "Want To Be Happy? Be Grateful", *TED Global,* 2013. https://www.ted.com/talks/david_steindl_rast_want_to_be_happy_be_grateful.

[69] Gordon Hempton, "Silence and the Presence of Everything", *On Being,* https://www.onbeing.org

[70] Hempton, *Silence.*

[71] Guidelines for Community Noise, *Who Int,* 1999. https://www.whoint/publications/i/item/a68672

[72] Eleanor Wachtel, "Colm Toibin", *Writers and Company,* CBC Radio, 2012.

[73] AAJ Staff, *The Role of Silence in Music,* https://www.allaboutjazz.com, 2005.

[74] Classic FM blog, "The most crushing, perfectly placed silences in classical music.", January 2016. https://www.classicfm.com.

[75] Passenger, "Whispers", *Whispers,* , (Black Crow, 2014).

[76] The Menil Collation, "*Silence*", Curator, Toby Kamps, 2012.

[77] Ashton Applewhite, "Let's End Ageism", *TED talk,* 2017. https://www.ted.com/talks/ashton_applewhite_let_s_end_ageism.

[78] David Suzuki, https://www.suzukielders.org.

[79] Suzuki, https://www.suzukielders.org

[80] Daniel Levitin, "The Keys to Aging Well", *Daily Good,* https://www.dailygood.org. 2021.

[81] Zalman Schacter-Salomi, *From Age-ing to Sage-ing: A Revolutionary Approach to Growing Older* (Balance, 2008), 6.

[82] Schacter-Salomi, *Age-ing,* 6.

[83] Schacter-Salomi, *Age-ing,* 37.

[84] Wallis, Velma, *Two Old Women* (HarperCollins Publishers, 1994).

[85] Plotkin, *Spiritual Ecology,* 208.

[86] Plotkin, *Spiritual Ecology,* 213.

[87] Thich Nhat Hanh, "Interrelationship", *Call Me By My True Names-The Collected Poems of Thich Nhat Hanh* (Parallex Press, 2005).

[88] David Hinton, "The Transformative Power of Landscape Practice", *Tricycle Magazine*, Summer, 2017.

[89] Levitin, *Successful Aging*, 37.

[90] John Robinson, *The Three Secrets of Aging: A Radical Guide* (Zero Books, 2012), 47.

[91] Robinson, *Three Secrets*, 60.

[92] Robinson, *Three Secrets*, 74.

[93] Schacter-Salomi, *Age-ing*, 216.

[94] Schacter-Salomi, *Age-ing*, 229.

[95] Plotkin, *Spiritual Ecology*, 211.

[96] Clarissa Pinkola Estes, *The Late Bloomer: Myths and Stories of the Wise Woman Archetype* (Sounds True, 2012).

[97] Molly Peacock, "Some Art Requires Living Long", *AARP Bulletin*, September, 2011.